PRAISE FOR FINANCE FASTTRACK

> It's always useful to read the wit and wisdom of Ken Langdon's and Alan Bonham's approach to business. If you want to build your confidence in debating issues with the finance department – this book is for you. It explains financial jargon, relates it to real business life and shows you how to use the financial side of your job to improve performance.

Martin Webb, Presenter of Channel 4's *Risking it All* and entrepreneur

> I like the way the book not only shows you how finance works but also explains how to use the financial side of business to build your career and aspire to the boardroom – an easy read of an irritatingly complicated topic.

Richard Humphreys, Former CEO Saatchi & Saatchi Advertising Worldwide and serial entrepreneur

FT

FAST TRACK TO SUCCESS

FINANCE

Prentice Hall

FINANCIAL TIMES

In an increasingly competitive world, we believe it's quality of
thinking that gives you the edge – an idea that opens new
doors, a technique that solves a problem or an insight that
simply makes sense of it all. The more you know, the smarter
and faster you can go.

That's why we work with the best minds in business and finance
to bring cutting-edge thinking and best learning practice to
a global market.

Under a range of leading imprints, including *Financial Times
Prentice Hall*, we create world-class print publications and
electronic products bringing our readers knowledge, skills and
understanding, which can be applied whether studying or at work.

To find out more about Pearson Education publications or tell us
about the books you'd like to find, you can visit us at
www.pearsoned.co.uk

PEARSON
Education

FAST TRACK TO SUCCESS
FINANCE

ALAN BONHAM AND KEN LANGDON

FT Prentice Hall
FINANCIAL TIMES

An imprint of Pearson Education

Harlow, England • London • New York • Boston • San Francisco • Toronto • Sydney • Singapore • Hong Kong
Tokyo • Seoul • Taipei • New Delhi • Cape Town • Madrid • Mexico City • Amsterdam • Munich • Paris • Milan

PEARSON EDUCATION LIMITED

Edinburgh Gate
Harlow CM20 2JE
Tel: +44 (0)1279 623623
Fax: +44 (0)1279 431059
Website: www.pearsoned.co.uk

First published in Great Britain in 2009

ISBN: 978-0-273-72178-9

British Library Cataloguing-in-Publication Data
A catalogue record for this book is available from the British Library

Library of Congress Cataloging-in-Publication Data
Bonham, Alan.
  Finance / Alan Bonham and Ken Langdon.
     p. cm.-- (Fast track to success)
  Includes bibliographical references and index.
  ISBN 978-0-273-72178-9 (pbk. : alk. paper) 1. Finance. I. Langdon, Ken. II. Title. III.
Title: Fast track to success : finance.
  HG173.B636 2009
  658.15--dc22
                            2009006236

10 9 8 7 6 5 4 3 2 1
13 12 11 10 09

Series text design by Design Deluxe
Typeset in 10/15 Swis Lt by 30
Printed and bound in Great Britain by Ashford Colour Press Ltd, Gosport, Hants

The publisher's policy is to use paper manufactured from sustainable forests.

CONTENTS

THE FAST TRACK WAY

Everything you need to accelerate your career

The best way to fast track your career as a manager is to fast track the contribution you and your team make to your organisation and for your team to be successful in as public a way as possible. That's what the Fast Track series is about. The Fast Track manager delivers against performance expectations, is personally highly effective and efficient, develops the full potential of their team, is recognised as a key opinion leader in the business, and ultimately progresses up the organisation ahead of their peers.

You will benefit from the books in the Fast Track series whether you are an ambitious first-time team leader or a more experienced manager who is keen to develop further over the next few years. You may be a specialist aiming to master every aspect of your chosen discipline or function, or simply be trying to broaden your awareness of other key management disciplines and skills. In either case, you will have the motivation to critically review yourself and your team using the tools and techniques presented in this book, as well as the time to stop, think and act on areas you identify for improvement.

Do you know what you need to know and do to make a real difference to your performance at work, your contribution to your company and your blossoming career? For most of us, the honest answer is 'Not really, no'. It's not surprising then that most of us never reach our full potential. The innovative Fast Track series gives you exactly what you need to speed up your progress and become a high performance manager in all the areas of the business that matter. Fast Track is not just another 'How to' series. Books on selling tell you how to win sales but not how to move from salesperson to sales manager. Project management software enables you to plan detailed tasks but doesn't improve the quality of your project management thinking and business performance. A marketing book tells you about the principles of marketing but not how to lead a team of marketers. It's not enough.

Specially designed features in the Fast Track books will help you to see what you need to know and to develop the skills you need to be successful. They give you:

→ the information required for you to shine in your chosen function or skill – particularly in the Fast Track top ten;

→ practical advice in the form of Quick Tips and answers to FAQs from people who have been there before you and succeeded;

→ state of the art best practice as explained by today's academics and industry experts in specially written Expert Voices;

→ case stories and examples of what works and, perhaps more importantly, what doesn't work;

→ comprehensive tools for accelerating the effectiveness and performance of your team;

→ a framework that helps you to develop your career as well as produce terrific results.

Fast Track is a resource of business thinking, approaches and techniques presented in a variety of ways – in short, a complete performance support environment. It enables managers to build careers from their first tentative steps into management all the way up to becoming a business director – accelerating the performance of their team and their career. When you use the Fast Track approach with your team it provides a common business language and structure, based on best business practice. You will benefit from the book whether or not others in the organisation adopt the same practices; indeed if they don't, it will give you an edge over them. Each Fast Track book blends hard practical advice from expert practitioners with insights and the latest thinking from experts from leading business schools.

The Fast Track approach will be valuable to team leaders and managers from all industry sectors and functional areas. It is for ambitious people who have already acquired some team leadership skills and have realised just how much more there is to know.

If you want to progress further you will be directed towards additional learning and development resources via an interactive Fast Track website **www.Fast-Track-Me.com**. For many, these books therefore become the first step in a journey of continuous development. So, the Fast Track approach gives you everything you need to accelerate your career, offering you the opportunity to develop your knowledge and skills, improve your team's performance, benefit your organisation's progress towards its aims and light the fuse under your true career potential.

ABOUT THE AUTHORS

ALAN BONHAM qualified as a chartered accountant and has since spent most of his time training others. He was a director at Anderson's Tutors Limited, where he prepared students for ICAEW exams. From there, he joined Neville Russell, where he became Training Manager. He then spent 16 years as a freelance lecturer and training consultant, specialising in audit and accounting topics.

Most recently, Alan was Director of Training for SWAT Ltd. As part of his role, he was responsible for the development of SWAT's national programme of CPD training, and he also presented a number of courses himself. He was Managing Director of Pentagon Training Ltd until the company was acquired by SWAT in October 2005.

Alan is now working again as a freelance lecturer – he is one of the few lecturers who can make auditing interesting. He also advises firms on their audit procedures and offers practical help in achieving compliance in a cost-effective manner. He has also worked with non-accountants and is the co-author of *Smart Things To Know About Business Finance*, which demystifies the language of finance.

E alanbonham@btinternet.com

KEN LANGDON has used his background in technology as a trainer and consultant to many of the major computer companies around the world. He has lectured in the USA, Australia and all over the Far East and Europe. In particular he has taught finance for non-financial managers and worked hard at explaining how the slightly esoteric world of finance reflects the real world of business. He is the author of a number of books on this and related topics.

E KPL@Pobox.com

A WORD OF THANKS FROM THE AUTHORS

We would like to thank the following for their generous contributions to this book:

→ **Liz Gooster, Pearson.** There are many exciting new ideas in the publishing world at present, but without an enthusiastic champion, most will simply die a slow death. Liz had the confidence to commission the Fast Track series and associated web-tool on behalf of the Pearson Group at a time when other publishers were cutting back on non-core activities. She has remained committed to its success – providing direction, challenge and encouragement as and when required.

→ **Ken Langdon.** As well as being a leading author in his own right, Ken has worked with all the Fast Track authors to bring a degree of rigour and consistency to the series. As each book has developed, he has been a driving force behind the scenes, pulling the detailed content for each title together in the background – working with an equal measure of enthusiasm and patience!

→ **Mollie Dickenson.** Mollie has a background in publishing and works as a research manager at Henley Business School, and has been a supporter of the project from its inception. She has provided constant encouragement and challenge, and is, as always, an absolute delight to work with.

→ **Critical readers.** As the Fast Track series evolved, it was vital that we received constant challenge and input from other experts and from critical readers.

→ **Professor David Birchall.** David has worked to identify and source Expert Voice contributions from international academic and business experts in each Fast Track title. David is co-author of the Fast Track *Innovation* book and a leading academic author in his own right, and has spent much of the last 20 years heading up the research programme at Henley Business School – one of the world's top ten business schools.

Our expert team

Last but not least, we are grateful for the contributions made by experts from around the world to each of the Fast Track titles.

EXPERT	TOPIC	BUSINESS SCHOOL/ COMPANY
Professor David Birchall	Challenges in organisational measurement – the example of innovation performance (p. 23)	Henley Business School, University of Reading
Professor Tony Julius and Professor Carole Print	The changing face of the finance function (p. 34)	Henley Business School, University of Reading
Professor Kiran Virdee and and Professor Carole Print	Financial planning and value creation (p. 81)	Henley Business School, University of Reading
Professor Carole Print	What is the financial value of people? (p. 98)	Henley Business School, University of Reading
Dr Giampiero Favato	Consortium stretches the limits of hostile takeover (p. 112)	Henley Business School, University of Reading
Dr Giampiero Favato	Value drivers of corporate deals (p. 131)	Henley Business School, University of Reading
Keith Baxter	ABCD quality based costing (p. 142)	Managing Director, De-Risk, Farnham

FINANCE FAST TRACK

Have you ever tried to argue with a finance director? They don't play fair. They have at their disposal a whole host of jargon calculated to wrong foot, not necessarily deliberately, any up and coming manager. Take managers, like you perhaps, newly promoted into facing new challenges. They are trained for the functional task to which they have been assigned but have no experience of the bunch of financial hurdles and measures that come with the job.

Much of this financial information they feel they ought to know, since they probably learnt the basics at college. Or perhaps they are finding it difficult to make the bridge from the basics at college to the real world of business they find themselves in. In fact they would actually understand some of this financial information if it had been expressed differently, using the same language they had been taught. It all appears to be a distraction from the job they want to do rather than a help in getting it done.

But it's a vicious circle. If you ignore the financial side of your job, you will start to lose control of the physical task. If you get behind with the administration, it's only going to get worse. If you do not query figures that appear to be wrong, particularly cross charges coming in from other parts of the business, you could find yourself having a huge load of costs dumped on you by someone who has learnt their way around the system and has seen you coming. Even if there is no one in your organisation with such evil intent, you must not rely on the internal costing systems, since they are very difficult to get right and are notoriously inaccurate. The difficulty is in making the systems keep up with changes in the organisation.

If this surprises you, you probably need to refresh yourself on the difference between financial accounts – the ones companies publish – and management accounts, which are meant to assist everyone to run the business and meet their objectives. You'll find this in Chapters 1 and 3 of this book. The point in the end, of course, concerns decision making. You can make a decision that seems correct for the organisation but is financially wrong, and vice versa. If you combine your functional skills with knowledge of the financial consequences of your decisions, you are on the way to being a Fast Track manager.

And, don't forget the finance director's array of jargon – believe it or not, you can have huge reserves on the balance sheet and no money in the bank. You can achieve a 20% return on capital employed and go bust at the same time.

Here is a simple example of a company whose profitability is unquestionable, but whose cash position threatens not only its ability to pay dividends but also its ability to survive. The company is making a healthy profit. In fact its return on capital employed at 20% is pretty good. There is nothing untoward either about its ability to pay its interest charges out of its profits. In fact, interest accounts for less than a third of its profits before interest and tax. Here are the numbers:

Long-term debt	60.0
Shareholders' funds	40.0
Capital employed	100.0
Return on capital employed	20%
Profit before interest and tax	20.0
Interest rate	8%
Interest	4.8
Profit before tax	15.2
Tax rate	30%
Tax	4.5
Net profit after interest and tax	10.7

Unfortunately these numbers only show one of the implications of debt, i.e. interest. Another one is making repayments. In this case the company has to pay back £12,000 a year on the five-year loan. Now look at the numbers:

Net profit after interest and tax (as before)	10.7
Repayments	12.0
Net cash outflow	−1.3

So, bad luck, they are making money and running out of cash.

Who is this book for?

If you are in the situation of the manager described above, this book is certainly for you. You are probably not a chartered accountant in the finance department, unless of course you are thinking of buying enough copies of the book to give to all the managers in production and sales, which could be good for business. (It would certainly be good for our business.) You may, however, be in a finance team and be looking to make progress by learning more about the financial side of business outside your particular function of, perhaps, credit control.

You could be in any other function – sales, marketing, production, engineering and even research and development – with responsibility for achieving results both functional and financial. To do this you need to understand finance, read annual reports and make clever use of spread-sheets. This book helps with all that, plus it helps you to understand how your company and team is performing. And it helps you when you have to deal with the finance people.

Perhaps you are in the public sector, in which case most of the financial tools and techniques used in the book will be relevant and usable. However, if your organisation has not adopted the International Financial Reporting Standards as yet, you will find the part about financial reporting only applicable to your customers and suppliers. You will, however, find that your organisation will have a plan to adopt those standards in the near future.

The book aims to demystify the finance function and give you the confidence to discuss business with accountants and finance directors. Financial people can be helpful if you know how to get the best out of them – and this book shows you how.

Don't forget that people with a tendency to blind you with science often get things wrong. Also remember that people who concentrate on only one element of running a business often lose touch with the big picture. We think this can be particularly true of some in finance.

One other argument for getting to grips with finance is that it helps you to accomplish your ambition for the future of the company and your team. Suppose you are trying to get more resources out of the big blue-chip company you work for because you can see a way of deploying them that will generate profit. Before you present your proposal, ask the appropriate finance person: 'What financial criteria do you use to decide whether a new project should go ahead or not?' If their killer response of 'We use a hurdle rate of 22%' leaves you wrong-footed, then this book will help you to continue that conversation and calculate the return on your project for yourself.

In summary:

→ Do you want to know enough about finance to be able to discuss matters with finance people or the finance director?

→ Is it high time you were able to make sense out of the financial pages in the newspapers?

→ Does your job require you to understand company reports – your own, or those of your suppliers, or those of customers?

→ Would it help you in your job if you understood the financial side of investment appraisal?

→ In time to come, might you need to understand how external finance is attracted into a project or business?

If the answer to any of these questions is 'Yes', then this is the book for you.

HOW TO USE THIS BOOK

Fast Track books present a collection of the latest tools, techniques and advice to help build your team and your career. Use this table to plan your route through the book.

PART	OVERVIEW
About the authors	A brief overview of the authors, their background and their contact details
A **Awareness**	*This first part gives you an opportunity to gain a quick overview of the topic and to reflect on your current effectiveness*
1 *Finance in a nutshell*	A brief overview of finance and a series of frequently asked questions to bring you up to speed quickly
2 *Finance audit*	Simple checklists to help identify strengths and weaknesses in your team and your capabilities
B **Business Fast Track**	*Part B provides tools and techniques that may form part of the finance framework for you and your team*
3 *Fast Track top ten*	Ten tools and techniques to help you implement a sustainable approach to finance and financial people based on the latest best practice
4 *Technologies*	A review of the latest technologies used to improve effectiveness and efficiency of financial activities
5 *Implementing change*	A detailed checklist to identify gaps and to plan the changes necessary to implement your framework for finance in your current position
C **Career Fast Track**	*Part C focuses on you, your leadership qualities and what it takes to get to the top*
6 *The first ten weeks*	Recommended activities when starting a new role with a financial element, together with a checklist of useful facts to know
7 *Leading the team*	Managing change, building your team and deciding your leadership style
8 *Getting to the top*	Becoming professional in all matters financial, getting promoted and becoming a director – what does it take?
D **Director's toolkit**	*The final part provides more advanced tools and techniques, based on industry best practice*
Toolkit	Advanced tools and techniques used by senior managers
Glossary	Glossary of terms

FAST-TRACK-ME.COM

Throughout this book you will be encouraged to make use of the companion site: **www.Fast-Track-Me.com**. This is a custom-designed, highly interactive online resource that addresses the needs of the busy manager by providing access to ideas and methods that will improve individual and team performance quickly. Top features include:

→ **Health Checks.** Self-audit checklists allowing evaluation of you and your team against industry criteria. You will be able to identify areas of concern and plan for their resolution using a personal 'Get-2-Green' action plan.

→ **The Knowledge Cube.** The K-Cube is a two-dimensional matrix presenting Fast Track features from all topics in a consistent and easy-to-use way – providing ideas, tools and techniques in a single place, anytime, anywhere. This is a great way to delve in and out of business topics quickly.

→ **The Online Coach.** The Online Coach is a toolkit of fully interactive business templates in MS Word format that allow Fast-Track-Me.com users to explore specific business methods (strategy, ideas, projects, etc.) and learn from concepts, case examples and other resources according to your preferred learning style.

→ **Business Glossary.** The Fast Track Business Glossary provides a comprehensive list of key words associated with each title in the Fast Track series, together with a plain English definition – helping you to cut through business jargon.

The website can also help answer some of the vital questions managers are asking themselves today (see figure on next page).

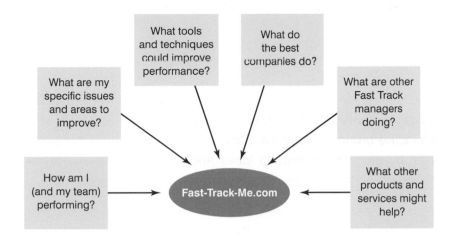

Don't get left behind: log on to **www.Fast-Track-Me.com** now to get your career on the fast track.

AWARENESS

This book introduces a sustainable approach to business finance aimed at keeping you, your team and your organisation at the forefront of financial planning, thus contributing towards the future of all three. The starting point is to gain a quick understanding of what business finance is and what it is not, and to be aware of your and your team's capabilities in this area right now. For this reason we will ask you a number of questions that will reveal where you and your team need to improve if you are truly to have a financially aware culture and meet the aims of business finance – a balance between achieving the organisation's objectives and producing the financial performance that the shareholders want, which is a company that is among the leaders in your industry.

'Know yourself' was the motto above the doorway of the Oracle at Delphi and is a wise thought. It means that you must do an open and honest self-audit as you start on the process of setting up your framework for finance.

The stakes are high. Business finance is at the heart of success in this global, competitive marketplace. Your team, therefore, needs to be effective financially and you need to be a good leader in understanding finance. Poor leadership in any part of the task and poor team effectiveness will make failure likely. An effective team poorly led will sap the team's energy and lead in the long term to failure through their leaving for a better environment or becoming less effective through lack of motivation. Leading an ineffective team well does not prevent the obvious conclusion that an ineffective team will not thrive. So, looking at the figure below, how do you make sure that you and your team are in the top right-hand box – an innovative and effective team with an excellent leader? That's what this book is about, and this section shows you how to discover your and your team's starting point.

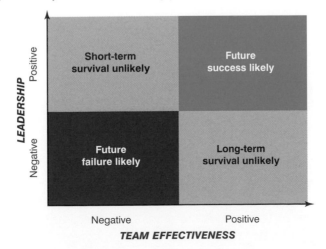

1

FINANCE IN A NUTSHELL

Starting with the basics

Just what is business finance?

Business finance, particularly if it is described as corporate finance, sounds complicated. But essentially it is:

→ the attraction of money into businesses and projects;

→ the monitoring of the ins and outs of money during operations;

→ the calculation and reporting of return, or profitability;

→ the use of figures to understand the health of a business and to decide what to do next.

These tasks have always described the role of finance, no matter what the current jargon and flavours of the month are. Indeed, one of the ways of dealing with financial matters is to push the problem back into one of these areas and get back to basics.

If you want proof that nothing in the financial world really changes, consider this. In one of the books in Galsworthy's *Forsyte Saga*, a board of directors is taking questions from the floor from investors attending a biggish company's 1891 annual general meeting. Much time was taken up with questions concerning a very small charitable donation that had been made by the company to an employee who had been injured at work. More than a hundred years later Ken, one of the authors of this book, was at the AGM of a large investment trust where there was a long discussion about a small donation that, for some reason, had been traditionally made by the company. It was to a Roman Catholic organisation and the chairman finished the item by simply declaring that the investment trust had always made the donation and that since he was a Roman Catholic he would continue the practice.

It just goes to show that finance baffles people into only asking questions on minor topics they can definitely understand. The Fast Track manager has to have enough knowledge to do a lot better than that.

If we analyse the purposes of financial reporting and list them in flow-chart form, the steps would be as follows:

1 Shareholders decide what businesses to invest in.

2 The board of directors raises funds from investors and lenders.

3 Senior managers decide what projects and deals to pursue to make the best return on the money in the business.

4 Senior managers decide short- and medium-term targets and budgets.

5 Managers use internal management accounts to check progress towards their targets and budgets.

6 Companies publish their half-yearly and annual reports to advise shareholders, lenders, customers and suppliers of their progress in the previous time period.

7 Commentators and investment advisers use the published information to make recommendations to new and existing investors.

A simplified version looks like this:

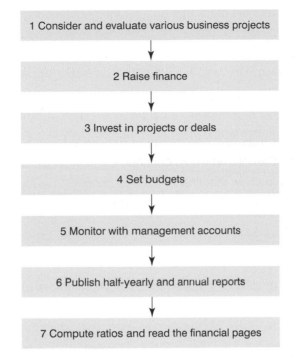

And from step 7 we go back to step 1 and the cycle starts again. Let's look at these steps one by one.

1 Shareholders decide what businesses to invest in

One of the threads running through business is that all businesspeople have in their minds a small number of ratios. They constantly monitor these performance measures to keep their job or business or part of a business on track. As we shall see, this is true of all businesspeople – from the one-person building contractor, to the first line manager in a multinational, to the board of directors.

So, what are the key ratios that the shareholders in a company look at and keep in mind as they decide whether to buy more shares, stay as they are or sell shares that they own?

The main question a potential investor asks is, 'Will this investment give me a better return than investing elsewhere, given the level of risk that I am happy to take?' Generally speaking, high return goes with high risk, so the potential shareholder needs data on a share that gives them some clues about whether to invest or not.

There are two main ratios that do this: the price/earnings ratio and the dividend yield. Both of these are published every working day in the financial pages of most newspapers.

The price/earnings ratio is calculated as share price/earnings per share. It gives an investor a picture of what the stock market expects from a company. In a nutshell, if the price/earnings is very high, say 30, then the market as a whole thinks that the company is going to grow fast but is relatively high risk. If it is low then the opposite is the case – a reliable though less adventurous company.

The dividend yield compares the price of a share, what the investor would have to pay today to buy a share and the historical dividend. This tells the investor what short-term return they will get on the share. They can compare this with interest rates for cash savings.

2 The board of directors raises funds from investors and lenders

The two sources of long-term finance in a business are share capital and loan capital. Share capital comes in as cash when the initial owners of the business first buy their shares. The owners will probably at the outset be the founders of the business and intrepid venture capitalists: either private, like the founder's dad and mum, or public, such as venture capital funds.

QUICK TIP ATTRACTING SHARE CAPITAL
Keep working hard to master the skills of business planning; they are difficult and take time to learn. Remember that to attract share capital into a new business, the board – which is where you want to be – needs above all things a credible business plan that promises a return commensurate with the risk of failure.

The implications of the two types of capital are different. In one sense share capital is cheaper. Return on the shareholders' capital comes in the shape of dividends that are normally paid twice a year. In the early stages of a business the owners may very well drop the requirement for dividends and allow the managers to keep all the profits in the business for expansion. At that stage the money could be said to be free. There is also no necessity for the managers to plan to have the cash to buy the shares back. In practical terms the money is in the company for ever.

The only downside in using share capital to get a business going is the cost of the operation: lawyers and accountants do not come cheap. And of course you have to find someone happy to take the risk of putting money into a business that may very well fail, with the consequent loss of the entire capital injection. It is this risk of failure that makes shareholders demand, in the long term, that their overall returns consisting of dividends and share price growth should be higher than the providers of loans.

Loan capital is probably cheaper to arrange. It comes from banks and financial institutions that measure the risk of the company and then charge an interest rate to reflect that risk. There is a huge irony here; the newer the business, the more it needs loan capital to generate its products before it sells them. But the newer the business, the higher the risk to the lender that they might not get their money back, so the higher the interest rate they charge.

3 Senior managers decide what projects and deals to pursue to make the best return on the money in the business

What senior managers have to do is look into the future – sometimes a long time into the future. They have to get into a position where they can convert estimates for business success into a convincing story of why one project should be preferred over another. For example, should they put more money into existing sales channels or try to break into a new market? They and eventually middle managers as well weigh up in advance the return they are going to make from each decision they take.

It's easy to get bound up in the interesting maths that go into the final part of making such a decision, but we must not ignore the fact that most business decisions are made on calculated assessments by experienced people, analysing what will occur if the business takes a certain course of action. The financial side is a great tool to assist decision making, but a decision-making tool should never be mistaken for the decision itself.

It is an interesting fact that when you are a manager you find that whenever a member of your team asks to see you, as opposed to you asking to see them, they are almost certainly going to ask for resources.

Your job as a manager or team leader is to gather the information you need to make a good decision on where to put resources.

The creation of a business case template is a good start to the investment appraisal process. It helps people know what management is looking for and ensures that new ideas conform with the company's overall strategy. The logical steps in the process are to estimate as accurately as possible the costs and benefits of investing in a project, weight them for risk and then use financial tools to make fair comparisons of one project with another.

4 Senior managers decide short- and medium-term targets and budgets

With the options before them and with management's best predictions on the return on each option, senior managers are in a position to decide what the business is going to do and how it will measure its success.

Probably after an annual or ad hoc review of the structure of the organisation, senior managers hand down the key performance indicators they will use to measure the success of each business unit. This leads to the setting of targets and budgets.

A budget is simply a plan. Strictly, a budget is a plan expressed in financial terms, but companies will, for example, produce budgets for material usage, manpower requirements and other resources as well as for accounting purposes. Indeed budgets that overemphasise the financial side can give much less help to the managers of the business than ones that take into account the physical side of running the business.

The budgeting system or cycle tends to be an annual ritual. However, such a narrow time-dependent focus can lead to horrible anomalies.

Budgets should achieve three objectives. They should:

→ assist in the company's planning process;

→ help in coordinating the activities of the various parts of the organisation;

→ enable the company to control its operations.

In addition, the budgetary process should be useful in forcing management to examine closely the operations of the company so that it can produce a viable budget.

5 *Managers use internal management accounts to check progress towards their targets and budgets*

Published financial accounting is concerned with the production of accounts, particularly for shareholders. The Companies Act in the UK governs the format of these accounts for unquoted companies – that is, companies not listed on the stock exchange. Quoted companies are subject to the rules and regulations set by the International Accounting Standards Board. Management accounts, on the other hand, are prepared in order to assist the managers of the business. There is no standard format, so they should be presented in the way that is most helpful in the particular circumstances of the company concerned. They should also contain sufficient detail to permit close control of the business.

Management accounts, therefore, have a very different role from financial accounts, and the time difference is enormous. Management accounts must give managers real-time information. It may be too late for some critical measures in some environments if information takes more than a week to get to the manager concerned. Fast Track managers pay a lot of attention to the management accounting system. After all, it is how senior managers judge their performance.

The point of management accounts is that they show the trends in a business – they are a rolling reading of what is going on in the business and they highlight the first signs of success or trouble.

6 *Companies publish their half-yearly and annual reports to advise shareholders, lenders, customers and suppliers of their progress in the previous time period*

Good business comes from innovation, risk and customer satisfaction. But it also needs some simple measures to keep control.

Businesses thrive in the end by selling products and services to markets. To sell products, you need first to produce them. To produce them, businesspeople need money up front. People with money are always looking for ways to invest their cash and earn a return. The limited company is the vehicle that brings these two things together.

Company legislation permits such companies to limit the liability of their shareholders to the nominal value of their shares. In effect, by applying for a £1 share, a shareholder agrees to subscribe £1 and is not liable for any further contribution in the event of the company's insolvency. This is unlike a partnership, where the partners, who own the business, are personally liable for all the partnership's liabilities.

Directors have to obey a set of rules in order to give a fair picture of the financial health of the enterprise. These are defined and developed by the government and the accounting standards bodies. The company's auditors use these standards to monitor the company by carrying out continuous and annual audits. In theory, and often in practice, the audit is a mechanism that gives shareholders and tax authorities confidence in the values that the board uses in the various financial documents it provides.

The board of directors is responsible for the stewardship of the owners' money. This stewardship involves the orderly recording of business transactions and the presentation of summary reports. This leads finally to the development of bookkeeping and accountancy.

Bookkeeping and accountancy have four main purposes:

→ to act as a check against fraud and error;

→ to assist managers with the information they need to make decisions;

→ to form the basis for accounting practices;

→ to produce standards of reporting that the owners and would-be owners of a company can use to judge its past performance.

Yet whatever mechanisms there are behind public companies, in the end shareholders entrust their money to company directors who are charged with using it effectively and efficiently.

Once the owners and lenders to the business have put cash into the company's bank, the company is free to start trading. It will need to spend some of the money on fixed assets – buildings, vehicles and so on – but the concentration of middle managers will be on working capital. This is the cash they use to create products and services, sell them and provide after-sales support. Their main measures come down, in the end, to how quickly the cash flows round this working capital cycle.

CASE STORY HEATING CONTRACTOR, TONY'S STORY

Narrator Tony, an engineer, is the chairman and majority shareholder of a small heating, air-conditioning and ventilation company.

Context For many reasons, anyone in the building trade is going to have a tight cash flow to run. Going bust is endemic in the industry, which causes high levels of bad debt. Contractors have to pay their people during the project and also their suppliers, while the customer pays on completion of agreed milestones and at the end of the project. Even then the customer may retain some money until the work has been thoroughly tested in a live environment.

Issue When Tony's company was heavily involved in projects and spending on labour and materials, money was very tight. When the business was less busy, the cash flowed in as customers paid their bills, and the owners were tempted to spend it on drawing salaries for themselves, outings for the staff and new offices and equipment.

Solution Tony realised that he and the other shareholders had to retain much more cash in the business even though their spending still left them very profitable. They decided to put by three months of overhead costs in the business at all times.

Learning This ebb and flow occurs, albeit less dramatically, in all businesses. Building up working capital is a necessary buffer against slower times.

The finance department of the enterprise regularly reports to the shareholders on progress during the preceding period. It may issue reports at the half-year stage or even on a quarterly basis, but the biggest interest and publicity is given to the annual report. As well as the board's predictions for the future of the company, the annual report contains three main financial statements: the income statement (also known as the profit and loss account), the balance sheet and the cash flow statement. These are covered in Chapter 3.

*7 Commentators and investment advisers use the published infor-
mation to make recommendations to new and existing investors*

Many people – shareholders, lenders, customers, suppliers and competitors, for example – are very interested in the financial ratios that
people use at corporate level to compare last year with this year, and
one business with another. So that we quickly get to the relevance and
usefulness of such ratios, we will start with a summary of the first four
types of ratio in which people are most interested. More detail is provided on the subject of ratios on page 170 in the Director's Toolkit.

→ **Liquidity.** Liquidity ratios measure the ability of a company to
pay its pressing debts. Companies owe their suppliers for
goods and services received, for example, and they have to
pay on time or risk not being re-supplied. If a company has
more cash than the sum of its short-term liabilities, it is said to
be liquid. If short-term debt is more than cash in hand, then a
company's liquidity can be in question.

→ **Profitability.** Everyone, perhaps shareholders in particular, is
interested in how profitable the company is, and they find this
information by using a number of profitability ratios. Perhaps
the simplest of these is the ratio of profit to sales. After calculating that ratio you can compare one company's profit
performance with that of its competitors.

→ **Gearing.** Gearing ratios show how much money the shareholders have in the business compared to its lenders – the
ratio of equity to loan capital. If a company has a low level of
debt when compared to the amount of equity, it is said to be
low-geared. Where there is a high level of debt compared to
equity, then the company is highly geared. A highly geared
company may be prepared to push for rapid growth and to
take more business risks to achieve this; or it could, of course,
be in trouble.

→ **Employee.** These ratios measure employee productivity. It can
be useful, for example, to compare what level of sales the
company is achieving with the number of staff it is employing.
If that figure is lower than that of a competitor, the company

can be said to be less productive. Where there is an indication that this might be the case, managers will concentrate on ways to improve productivity.

> **QUICK TIP FORM YOUR OWN BENCHMARK**
> When you look at the financial ratios of different industries, look particularly at the differences. For example, build a benchmark of what is good liquidity in the retail industry as opposed to the aerospace industry.

Why is finance so important?

Ken once ran a long series of finance courses for non-financial managers for the whole salesforce of a big company. About halfway through he asked the sales director whether there were any differences in the sales-force as they went about their selling after they had attended the course compared to before. The sales director's reply was a thoughtful one. After a pause he said, 'The whole operation is simply more professional. They do sometimes ask probing questions about how their customers will judge financial viability, and they certainly make much more use of the annual reports of their main customers, but I think the main benefit is that they are more confident and professional businesspeople.'

That's a good summary of why the finance topic is so important – you cannot really be a businessperson if you do not have an understanding of the financial side that is at least good enough to give you the confidence to ask financial questions and seek out financial knowledge. No matter what your team is trying to achieve, they will operate better if they understand the financial consequences of what they are doing. We can look at examples from every part of the business.

A typical research and development (R&D) department has an almost infinite list of opportunities that they could examine and put resources into. They will make those resource decisions based on competitive pressures, customer needs, market trends and so on; but if they do not also examine the financial possibilities and opportunities of all the options, they are missing out one of the most important criteria in their decision making. Difficult though it may be to make estimates of sales as a result of new features on their products, they have to do it. Not only that, but they also have to use financial techniques to make it possible to compare two or more potential projects with very different characteristics. In short, finance allows you to compare apples with pears and improve your chances of making the right choice.

Think about a sales team – their job is to make profitable sales, not just to make sales. Yes, they use loss leaders from time to time to gain strategic advantage, but a reasonable knowledge of finance will ensure that they are making an informed choice when they sell a loss leader, not just lowering the price at any cost to make the sale.

So, don't be put off by the technicalities of business finance. In the end it comes back to the basics – get money into the business and decide where to invest it, monitor the money as it goes in and out, calculate the profitability of the enterprise and use those calculations to work out what to do next.

So why is it so difficult – what typically goes wrong?

1 **The system has unforeseen consequences.** When setting up profit centres it is normally necessary for notional money to move from one manager's profit and loss account to another's; for example, in a garage when the service department works on a car that the sales department is about to sell, it will charge sales for the work. This can have unfortunate repercussions if it is not done carefully – the internal system forces managers to make decisions that are in the interests of their department but not in the least in the interests of the whole company.

2 **People confuse revenue with profit.** Here's an example from the salesforce: 'Sorry, mate, I've found a cheaper quote.' What does your salesforce do when it hears these words? If they generally come straight back to managers asking for permission to give a discount, you have a problem – the salespeople have indicated to the customer that there is room for manoeuvre on price rather than showing confidence in the added benefits of their solution. There is often a simple reason that salespeople

do this – they do not understand how a small discount on the sales price produces an inordinately big impact on the bottom line. Take this example from the insurance industry. This has always been a price-sensitive business. Intermediaries and even consumers, who can use the internet, can trawl for the cheapest price. The figures below graphically demonstrate the impact on the bottom line of giving away any of the commission percentage the broker earns from a sale:

Premium	£1,000
Cost of insurance	£800
Gross margin	£200
Expenses	£50
Net profit	£150

Here is a sale ruined by discounting commissions. The original commission rate is 20%. This gives the gross margin on £1,000 as £200. Under pressure, the salesperson gives a 10% discount. The bottom line has decreased by 66%:

Premium	£900
Cost of insurance	£800
Gross margin	£100
Expenses	£50
Net profit	£50

This is a brilliant example of the absolute necessity of a team understanding the financial implications of what they are doing.

3 **The financial information you are getting is too late, incomprehensible or plain wrong.** This is more frequently the case than most finance directors make out. If the numbers you get on a regular basis do not help you to run your team, complain. Explain what you want, listen to why you are not getting it at the moment and get them to change the system – or, at worst, extract another subset of the stuff you actually need on a special-case basis.

QUICK TIP THE BOARD BELIEVES THE FIGURES
Remember that even if your manager is aware that the internal system is not giving a proper statement of your results, the people above them will take the figures as gospel.

4 **Your financial controller does not understand your part of the business well enough.** Another common problem: you need some give and take here. Forming a good relationship with your financial controller works both ways. You can learn a lot from them about finance and how your organisation handles it, but you need to reciprocate by summing up how your business works and really showing them round.

5 **Shareholders make poor decisions on which companies to invest in.** The problem here is that the past is not necessarily a good guide to the future. The figures available to investors are last year's performance. Along with statements from the directors about their expectations for the future, this is the best information an outsider can have, but it still does not guarantee success.

6 **The board attempts to raise funds for investors and fails, or it does it at a high cost.** It never rains but it pours. Although the share price does not normally have any impact on the company itself, it does affect its ability to raise more money from investors and lenders. In difficult times the share price goes down, making it difficult or impossible to raise funds from investors. Also during troubled times interest rates normally go up, making the cost of borrowing higher.

7 **Managers present overoptimistic claims for projects they want to prove are viable.** If you look at any small start-up company's first business plan, it is always too optimistic on the top line of the profit and loss account – sales. It happens in large companies too. It is all too easy to start from the costs of a potential project and put down a sales figure that makes sure the project meets the criteria for a financially feasible plan.

8 The marketing and public relations departments blind us with glitz. The average annual report is now over 100 pages long, with glossy pictures of happy employees all over the world producing environmentally friendly products. They work with charities and support the local community. The company saves whales, is reducing its carbon footprint and treats its employees like kings and queens. If you only read the text and pictures part of an annual report, you could be forgiven for wondering whether the managers ever get round to trying to make any money. But the financial figures towards the back are harder to spin – and so we must become skilled at reading and interpreting them.

So just what is finance? – frequently asked questions

The following table provides quick answers to some of the most frequently asked questions about the topic of finance. Use this as a way of gaining a quick overview.

FAQ 1 *Is it possible to pick up a company's annual report and within ten minutes know what its principal products and markets will be during the next 12 months?*	1 Yes. It will take a little longer to start with, but with practice you will find that information in the chairman's statement and the reports of the other directors. In fact you don't have to pick the annual report up – you can find it on the company's website.
FAQ 2 *How do I test whether a company's published strategy is financially viable?*	2 You know the company strategy from reading the directors' reports in the annual report. This will give you some idea of the cash they will need to proceed. From the cash flow document and the balance sheet you can roughly see how easy or difficult it will be to support the strategy.
FAQ 3 *What are the most popularly quoted measures of profitability and liquidity?*	3 There are a number of each, but the most popular are return on capital employed (ROCE) and the current ratio. ROCE is a measure of how much profit the company is making compared with the amount of money put in by shareholders and lenders. The current ratio is the ratio of current assets (typically inventory, accounts receivable and cash) to current liabilities (e.g. the amounts owed to creditors). The current ratio is the most common test of the company's ability to meet its short-term commitments. All small business owners use the current ratio, whether they know it or not. They all know how much their customers owe them, how much they owe their suppliers and employees, and how much money they have in the bank.

FAQ 4 *Can I calculate these popular measures of financial health from the financial information published in an annual report, such as the income statement and balance sheet?*	4 You certainly can, and it's a good idea to do so. If you rely on what the company publishes you may be misled, because they will use whatever ratios suit them to produce the rosiest picture of the business.
FAQ 5 *How do I explain to a non-financial manager how a company or division can be making a satisfactory return on investment but still be in danger of financial collapse?*	5 You will just have to teach them about cash flow. In many ways it is better to plan the future of profit centres by looking at their cash flows rather than their profitability. It may be necessary to pass down targets on cash flow, such as giving an incentive to salespeople to get their customers to pay their bills fast.
FAQ 6 *Can I access on the internet figures that enable me to compare a company's financial measures with an industry average?*	6 Yes, you can, and it is a very useful facility. Try www.accountingweb.co.uk/icc. There are many other sites you can find with Google.
FAQ 7 *How do I refresh the knowledge I am gaining so that I don't forget how, for example, to do financial analysis?*	7 The quickest way is probably to read the financial pages of a newspaper. Many people find they benefit from reading the *Financial Times* one day a week, particularly on Saturday. It exposes them to financial jargon and, as a useful by-product, has a lot of personal finance information that day.
FAQ 8 *Which figures in a report and in accounts are written to a global standard?*	8 All quoted companies in the European Economic Area prepare their accounts using international standards. It is therefore possible to make comparisons between all such companies, safe in the knowledge that they have prepared their accounts using the same rules. In fact, about one hundred countries around the world follow international standards – although, as yet, this is not the case for companies in the USA.
FAQ 9 *What is the significance of the words the auditors use when giving their opinion of the financial figures of the company in question?*	9 In the grand majority of cases the auditors' report follows a standard format, indicating that the accounts are 'true and fair' and have been prepared in accordance with the rules. When, however, auditors modify their opinion by expressing some concerns, it is likely that something is badly wrong.

FAQ 10 *If I want to buy a company, will the balance sheet tell me what the company is worth?*	**10** No. The balance sheet tells you what the company owns and what it owes, but those assets and liabilities are included in the balance sheet at an amount based on accounting principles and not on market value. Further, when buying a business, you would often need to pay more than the value of the separate assets (less liabilities) because of factors such as contacts with customers, experience of staff, etc. The value of such assets is not included in the balance sheet. The premium that you would pay on top of the value of the net assets is known as goodwill.
FAQ 11 *How do I go through a logical process to compare one potential project or business opportunity with another?*	**11** You make a detailed estimate of the financial costs and benefits of the projects you are comparing, and when they will occur. You then adjust them for risk and contingency and apply financial tools such as discounted cash flows. All this will provide a useful pointer towards which project you should prefer.
FAQ 12 *How do I make sure that project opportunities have strategic fit?*	**12** First, express your strategy simply in terms of what products you will sell to what markets. This tells you which product/markets are the keys to the business in the future. Look at your project opportunities and you will be able to see which ones fit that strategy best.
FAQ 13 *How do you define and use the technique of discounted cash flows?*	**13** A discounted cash flow (DCF) compares the financial implications of different projects. Time is important here; money spent now is more valuable than money spent in the future, while income received now is also more valuable than income received in the future. A DCF recognises that fact and gives you a time-adjusted value of each project. Make sure you have plotted income and expenditure along a timeline and then use the DCF calculator in a spreadsheet.
FAQ 14 *How much does a company get when someone buys its shares on the stock exchange?*	**14** The company only gets benefit from a share transaction if the share being bought is a new share, either from the very first investors in the company or when the company goes to investors for new money. The grand majority of shares on the stock exchange are second hand, where a buyer, normally through a stockbroker, buys from an existing investor and the company gets no benefit.

FAQ 15 How do you distinguish relevant costs and income to put into an investment appraisal model?	**15** Relevant costs are those that will only occur if you decide to implement a project. So, for example, if a project uses resources you have already paid for, you do not include their costs in the investment appraisal calculation. Similarly, only allow income to be claimed by a project if it is strictly earned by that project.
FAQ 16 Is there any access to useful investment advice on the internet?	**16** More than you could ever use. If you Google 'investment appraisal' you will get lots of hits. The most useful ones are likely to be by practitioners rather than academics or finance people. Practitioners have experience of using the techniques in real life and on real projects – and that can be helpful.
FAQ 17 Can I understand financial terminology well enough to converse with a finance director?	**17** Yes and no. It is easy enough to bone up on the basics, but financial directors see the world through a different prism, so take it very slowly and repeatedly ask them to explain what they are saying to make sure that there are no misunderstandings.
FAQ 18 How do I take cultural differences into account when implementing a return on investment process?	**18** If you are doing an investment appraisal on a global basis, be very careful. On a line-by-line basis check that nomenclature is common to all the countries and that local managers have agreed with your estimate, particularly of income from the project. Only they will really know how realistic the estimates are for their countries. The best way is to have a standard way of doing such appraisals and make it available on the company intranet, so that people all over the world can use it.
FAQ 19 How do you build a cash flow from an income statement?	**19** This is quite simple. Strip out all non-cash items from the income statement. The most common of these is depreciation. Depreciation of fixed assets is charged as an expense in the income statement over the life of the asset. In the cash flow statement, the cash used to purchase the asset is shown as an expense at the start of the project.
FAQ 20 Is it worth learning how to use spreadsheets in an advanced way when you can simply go to the IT department and get them to do it?	**20** Yes, it is worth it. The point of spreadsheets is that the person raising the sheet is the same person who has a problem to solve. If you do it yourself, you are much more likely to get exactly what you want.

Tip

QUICK TIP VALUE A COMPANY BY ITS PROFITS
Always remember that the real value of a company depends on its future profits. It is from those future profits that shareholders will get their return, in the form of dividends.

Challenges in organisational measurement – the example of innovation performance

Professor David Birchall

Professor David Birchall

EXPERT VOICE

The importance to organisations of measuring performance is without question. The old adage is still relevant – 'If you can't measure it, you can't manage it'. Yet while much time and effort has been expended in developing measures to assess organisational activities, there seems to be little agreement about what should be measured and how. And the paucity of sound models of the organisational processes means there is also little agreement about how this measurement might inform actions to improve performance.

Traditional performance metrics used by organisations are decidedly weighted in favour of optimisation rather than progression and generally encourage a 'more of the same' environment for doing business. Also, it is often said that we have a 'measurement crisis',[1] which is the result of organisations 'drowning in data'. It is not so much that the wrong things are being measured but that too much is being measured, and that too great an attempt is being made to quantify features which do not really lend themselves usefully to quantification. The costs of measurement schemes are increasing, but are organisations and their executives getting better value? Is measurement leading to improved decision making? In fact, if measures are not well designed, they encourage behaviours that are not beneficial to the enterprise, so they actually become dysfunctional.

During downturns in the economy attention sensibly gets turned to cost saving. However, while cost saving must be a priority, care needs to be taken not to jeopardise the long term. Decisions have to be made about what activities to curtail or abandon, what to retain in-house and what to subcontract or outsource, and which locations to maintain and which to move out of. Often, decisions seem to be taken purely on cost criteria. Although it is vital for all areas of the organisation to justify themselves, it is important to remember that this will not be easy for those involved in activities with only a long-term pay-off.

As businesses sense a move in market conditions and an upturn, they will refocus on business building and innovative new offerings that are attractive to the market. Innovation will again become a key challenge, as

---

[1] Birchall, D.W. and Tovstiga, G. (2005), *Capabilities for Strategic Advantage: Leading Through Technological Innovation*, Basingstoke: Palgrave.

firms seek to differentiate themselves from competitors. But short-term deci-sions can seriously impact on a later ability to innovate. R&D in many firms becomes a target for cost reduction, and those involved in innovation will be under the spotlight to demonstrate its value. This is just one area where measurement proves illusive. Others include training and development, and capital investment in infrastructure, whether buildings or IT systems. Many areas can be delayed without too much grief, but this is less the case with much innovation activity. Once curtailed it easily gets lost, due to the loss of those with key skills who take with them much tacit knowledge.

The area of innovation has been taken to illustrate the challenges presented to those seeking to measure and manage performance. The work is based on a study of innovation performance measurement carried out at Henley,[2] and the results have been used to develop a framework for executive action.

Innovation is a multi-dimensional process, normally involving consider-able change across the organisation. Such processes do not lend themselves readily to measurement. The inputs to the process, whether based on in-company research or new knowledge appropriated from out-side the firm, are not readily related to outputs in the form of 'successful' new products or services. Even the impact of outputs from single innovation activities within an organisational setting do not lend themselves readily to being isolated, traceable and measurable within the overall portfolio of the firm's activities. Contributions from R&D to profitability in most firms are not readily attributable with any real sense of validity and reliability in the short term, and certainly, in today's complex world, not even in the long term. The development of a firm's capabilities to innovate is seen as paramount in cre-ating potential competitive advantage,[3] but these capabilities, based to a large degree on learning, no more lend themselves to quantitative measure-ment than the many other aspects of the innovation process and outcomes.

This research has shown that managers trying to find a way of measuring innovation performance are faced with a set of dilemmas, many of which are interrelated. These are shown below:

Measurement focused on innovation as incremental change	Measurement focused on innovation as radical change
Measurement for control	Measurement for learning
Innovation process focus	Innovation outcomes focus
To support decision making in the short term	Looking at long-term impact
Framework based on simple metrics	Elaborate system based on fine-grained measurement

[2] Birchall, D.W. and Tovstiga, G. (2005), *Innovation Performance Measurement in Organisations*, Henley-on-Thames: Henley Management College.
[3] Neely, A. (2004), 'Performance measurement: the new crisis', in S. Crainer and D. Dearlove (eds), *Financial Times Handbook of Management*, Harlow: Pearson Education.

Emphasis on quantifiable metrics	Emphasis on qualitative attributes
Precise definition of costs of innovation	Broad view of impact
Internal focus in measurement	External (customer) focus
Measures designed for and tailored to the specific situation	Organisation-wide measurement for comparison purposes
Narrow (departmental) focus	Organisation-wide view
Project focus	Portfolio approach
Internal review	External comparisons
Stage-gate reviews	Standard review periods
Minimising costs of administration	Quality, reliability and validity of measurement
Quality of innovation process	Quality and quantity of outputs

These dilemmas may well not be apparent to executives when making decisions about individual measures or approaches. Many relate to the assumptions underpinning decision making in organisations, the nature of management actions and its impact on behaviour.

Our framework can assist executives in thinking through decisions either in the design of an innovation performance approach tailored to the needs of the organisation or in an examination of the applicability of the existing approach. More importantly, the framework can be adapted to other areas where quantitative measures fail to give a full enough picture for decision making. 🙷

EXPERT VOICE

FINANCE AUDIT

To improve performance, you first need to understand your starting point – what your strengths and weaknesses are in the finance area and how each will promote or limit what you can achieve. There are two levels of awareness you need to have. The first is to understand what the most effective teams or businesses look like, how they behave and how near your team is to emulating them. The second is to understand what it takes to lead such a team – do you personally have the necessary attributes for success?

Team assessment

Is my team making best use of its financial knowledge?

Use the following checklist to assess the current state of your team, considering each element in turn. (You would use a different checklist to measure individual abilities within their function: this checklist is designed just to look at the financial strengths and weaknesses of the group.) Use a simple Red-Amber-Green evaluation, where Red reflects areas where you feel strongly that the statement is not correct in your organisation and there are significant issues requiring immediate attention. Amber suggests areas of concern and risk. Green means that you are happy with the current state.

ID	CATEGORY	EVALUATION CRITERIA	STATUS
Finance			RAG
F1	Strategic fit	The team understands how the performance of our department fits into the corporate vision, strategy and goals	☐
F2	KPI relevance	The achievement of departmental key performance indicators (KPIs) ensures our contribution to the achievement of corporate goals	☐
F3	KPI commitment	Each member of the team understands their individual KPIs and is totally committed to their achievement	☐
F4	Basic knowledge	Each member of the team understands the basics of business finance – cash flow, the income statement and, if necessary, the balance sheet	☐
F5	Budgeting	The team is involved in producing the budget and is committed to working within it	☐
F6	Financial research	The team uses information interpreted from the annual reports of key customers, competitors and suppliers	☐
F7	Project evaluation	The team understands how to build a business case using the organisation's template	☐
F8	Management accounting system	The team understands the internal financial information that we get and uses it to monitor our performance. Where the information system is weak we have in place a plan to get the system improved	☐
F9	Relationship with finance department	Our financial controller understands our part of the business and we regularly keep them up to date with key changes in our environment	☐
F10	Analytic tools	The team understands risk and breakeven analysis sufficiently to inform decision making	☐

QUICK TIP CONTROL

Make sure the management accounting system concentrates on as small a number of KPI measures as possible, so that you can control all of them with ease.

Having identified where the gaps are in your business or team capabilities, you need to understand whether you have the right skills and knowledge to be leading the team as their financial champion.

📖 **CASE STORY FERRY OPERATOR, MOHAMMED AND ALFIAN'S STORY**

Narrators Mohammed and Alfian were two would-be entrepreneurs who were backed by family money and looking for a new project.

Context Mohammed and Alfian wanted to offer a ferry service on the Thames for City commuters. Their unique selling proposition was that it would have a gym on board so that commuters could do a work-out while they were travelling to work.

Issue They were under pressure from the seller of a second-hand ferry to buy it quickly. Enthusiastically, the men worked out how they would cost the refit of the boat and were about to sign contracts to buy it, even though the rest of the business plan was sketchy.

Solution A friend of theirs urged them not to sign up until they at least knew how many passengers they would need to cover the costs of running the ferry. They did a breakeven analysis, despite the pressure from the seller, and found that it was not feasible to get enough passengers to pay the price they needed to cover their costs. Meanwhile, despite the urgency implied, the seller had still not sold the boat when this financial plan was complete.

Learning When you are very eager to do something in business, make sure you do the financial plan before taking on any commitments. Don't let your passion rule your head.

Self-assessment

Do I have what it takes?

This section presents a self-assessment checklist of the factors that make a successful Fast Track leader in finance. These reflect the knowledge, competencies, attitudes and behaviours required to get to the top, irrespective of your current level of seniority. Take control of your career, behave professionally and reflect on your personal vision for the next five years. This creates a framework for action throughout the rest of the book.

Use the checklist overleaf to identify where you personally need to gain knowledge or skills. Fill it in honestly and then get someone who knows you well – your boss or a key member of your team – to go over it with you. Be willing to change your assessment if people give you insights into yourself that you had not taken into account.

Use the following scoring process:

0 A totally new area of knowledge or skills

1 You are aware of the area but have low knowledge and/or lack skills

2 An area where you are reasonably competent and working on improvement

3 An area where you have a satisfactory level of knowledge and skills

4 An area where you are consistently well above average

5 You are recognised as a key figure in this area of knowledge and skills throughout the business

Reflect on the lowest scores and identify those areas that are critical to success. Flag these as status Red, requiring immediate attention. Then identify those areas that you are concerned about and flag those as status Amber, implying areas of development that need to be monitored closely. Status Green implies that you are satisfied with the current state.

ID	CATEGORY	EVALUATION CRITERIA	SCORE	STATUS
Knowledge			0–5	RAG
K1	Financial information	I have a thorough understanding of the basics of business finance – income statement, balance sheet, cash flow statement	☐	☐
K2	Investment appraisal	I know how to produce a business case using financial techniques such as discounted cash flow	☐	☐
K3	Management accounting	I know enough about the management accounting system to be able to explain it to team members and to get it adjusted to become more supportive in achieving my goals	☐	☐
K4	Team development	I understand human resources policies and procedures well enough to be able to support team members in their salary and career aspirations	☐	☐

ID	CATEGORY	EVALUATION CRITERIA	SCORE	STATUS
Competencies			0–5	RAG
C1	Organisational research	I am able in 10 minutes on an organisation's website to determine their product and market strategies	☐	☐
C2	Financial research	I am able within 10 minutes to produce the financial ratios from an annual report that will allow me to compare one organisation with another and with their industry average	☐	☐
C3	Risk analysis	I can use a process to assess risk, and produce optimistic, most likely and pessimistic estimates of the financial impact of a decision as an aid to decision making	☐	☐
C4	Making it happen	I can present a business case persuasively, both for promoting a project and adjusting my KPIs and management information needs	☐	☐
Attitudes				
A1	Cost consciousness	I spend the organisation's money as though it were my own. I constantly look for areas to cut costs and increase revenues. When I spend extravagantly it is for a well-defined purpose	☐	☐
A2	Key performance indicators	I am driven by my KPIs but I'm always aware of when achieving them may not be in the organisation's interests. When that happens, I strive to change them	☐	☐
A3	Balanced leadership	While being committed to achieving my objectives, I am well aware that allowing myself to get behind with financial and administrative matters will ultimately lower my performance	☐	☐
A4	Relationship with finance	I work on my relationship with finance and believe that the finance people are a valuable source of support in achieving my objectives	☐	☐

ID	CATEGORY	EVALUATION CRITERIA	SCORE	STATUS
Behaviours				
B1	Self-development	I read the business pages of a good quality newspaper on a regular basis. I keep up with developments in my industry and the industries of my customers (internal or external)	☐	☐
B2	Leadership	I have frequent one-to-one contact with my team members. I understand them well, not only in a work context but also in their personal life aspirations	☐	☐
B3	Career	I review my personal development plan regularly and work hard on mapping my route to my next promotion	☐	☐
B4	Commitment	I demonstrate enthusiasm to the team and a determination to achieve all KPIs	☐	☐

QUICK TIP FINANCIAL ANALYSIS

Don't rely on other people to analyse the financial impact of your decisions. They have a different agenda and may not have your interests primarily in mind.

QUICK TIP READ THE RIGHT THING

Read the technical magazines that are of interest to your customers as much as the ones that are of interest to you.

Audit summary

Take a few minutes to reflect on the leadership–team effectiveness matrix opposite and consider your current position: where are you and what are the implications?

→ **Bottom left – poor leadership and an ineffective team.** This will result in failure: who knows, you may already be too late.

→ **Top left – great leadership but a poor team.** You have a great vision but will be unlikely to implement it, and so it will have little impact. You will need to find a way of taking people with you and introducing systems and processes to improve team effectiveness.

→ **Bottom right – poor leadership but a great team.** You are highly effective and efficient as a team but may well be going in the wrong direction through poor leadership.

→ **Top right – clear leadership and direction combined with an efficient and effective team.** This is where we want to be. Lots of great new ideas for finance linked to current business goals and with a team unit capable of delivering on time and within budget. You don't need this book – please give it to someone else!

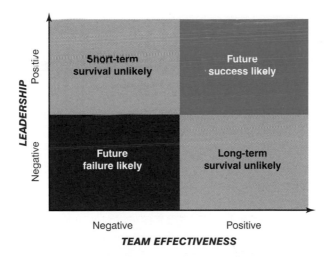

QUICK TIP LEADER RECOGNITION

Make sure that your leadership skills are referred to in your appraisal by preparing reasons that will encourage your boss to make positive comments on them. It is always more convincing to have someone else say how good you are in that area, rather than you having to bring the topic up.

STOP – THINK – ACT

Once you have completed the individual and team audits, take time to reflect on your profile so you can:

→ identify any 'quick wins' you could achieve today;
→ use the rest of the book effectively.

Reflect on the profiles of the team and yourself that you have produced. Ask yourself and the team these questions:

What should we do?	What will we change today and what difference will it make (why)?
Who do we need to involve?	Who else needs to be involved to make it work and why?
What resources will we require?	What information, facilities, materials, equipment or budget will be required and are they available?
What is the timing?	When will this change be implemented – is there a deadline?

Visit **www.Fast-Track-Me.com** to use the Fast Track online planning tool.

The changing face of the finance function

Professor Tony Julius and Professor Carole Print

One of the key roles of a finance function is to prepare and communicate information to managers and shareholders to show in monetary terms the economic resources of the business that are under the control of the management. In many organisations the role of the finance function has been under scrutiny in recent times, particularly when reviewing how it adds value beyond its traditional transactional activities – what is often described as the change from 'scorekeeper' to 'business partner'. Changes in the way finance functions are organised and the role they play require new relationships, contributions and structures. These provide significant challenges for those working in the finance function and responsible for it, who recognise the need to redefine their role to meet the needs of senior executives. These requirements can be summarised as:

→ maintaining control and integrity of company financial information;

→ managing financial risk;

→ challenging managers and helping them to create value;

→ supporting performance improvement and company-wide change.

As a result of pressure to balance the cost of the function and the value it provides, many finance functions have been substantially reduced through shared services and outsourcing of transaction processing, while maintaining effective control in line with ever changing governance requirements. At the same time, there are challenges to demonstrate the value the function provides to the business and to identify profitable growth opportunities. Recent research, involving finance executives at a number of large UK companies, has explored the role that finance plays, the factors impacting the future of the finance function and the barriers to change.[1] Their views are summarised below.

→ **The role that finance plays.** To a varied extent, finance functions are moving into more non-transactional areas. They are enabling businesses to become more global through maintaining accountability and consistent performance measures. While finance remains central to the integrity of organisations, business partnering is becoming the expected norm. There is a blurring around the edges of the role of finance. Rather than managing the traditional finance processes, the finance function is increasingly becoming an enabler across the organisation's functions and value chain, taking on the role of creation and execution of strategy, cost management, resource allocation, process design, risk monitoring and corporate governance. In an increasingly regulated environment, finance must also deal with larger volumes of data and with greater complexity while reducing its own costs. This has led to fragmentation of the function, with efficient transaction processing performed in shared service centres and business partners focusing on value effectiveness.

→ **The factors that will impact the future finance function.** Factors specific to individual organisations will continue to influence the structure and responsibilities of the finance function internally. However, the key external drivers for change are increased regulation, globalisation and increased competition.

---

[1] At Henley Business School, University of Reading.

→ **The barriers for change in the finance function.** The main barriers to change were identified as high workload, the distraction of further regulation and staff issues. The key enabler was perceived to be good systems.

The finance function of the future is expected to be shaped by four key drivers of change:

→ technology

→ globalisation

→ competition

→ an increasingly rigorous regulatory environment.

Profit in the future will increasingly result from exploiting the competitive advantage of intangible assets, which are not captured fully in a traditional finance system.

In future, businesses will look to their finance functions to manage increased regulation and complexity. At the same time, as organisations become more global, competition more fierce and the requirement for change faster, the value-adding role provided by the business partnering aspects of the finance function will become more important.

BUSINESS
FAST TRACK

Irrespective of your chosen function or discipline, look around at the successful managers whom you know and admire. We call these people Fast Track managers, people who have the knowledge and skills to perform well and fast track their careers. Notice how they excel at three things:

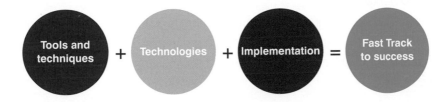

Tools and techniques

They have a good understanding of best practices for their particular field. This is in the form of methods and techniques that translate knowledge into decisions, insights and actions. They understand what the best companies do and have an ability to interpret what is relevant for their own businesses. The processes they use are generally simple to explain and form a logical step-by-step approach to solving a problem or capturing data and insights. They also encourage creativity – Fast Track managers do not follow a process slavishly where they know they are filling in the boxes rather than looking for insights on how to improve performance. This combination of method and creativity produces the optimum solutions.

They also have a clear understanding of what is important to know and what is simply noise. They either know this information or have it at their fingertips as and when they require it. They also have effective filtering mechanisms so that they don't get overloaded with extraneous information. The level of detail required varies dramatically from one situation to another – the small entrepreneur will work a lot more on the knowledge they have and in gaining facts from quick conversations with experts, whereas a large corporate may employ teams of analysts and research companies. Frequently when a team is going through any process they uncover the need for further data.

Technologies

However, having the facts and understanding best practice will achieve little unless they are built into the systems that people use on a day-to-day basis. Fast Track managers use appropriate technologies to maximise both effectiveness and efficiency.

Implementation

Finally, having designed the framework that is appropriate to them and their team, Fast Track managers are also great at implementation, putting in place the changes necessary to build and sustain the performance of the team.

In the next chapters we will outline the structures and processes that cover all these topics, but the choice as to how tightly or loosely you will use them will vary, and will to a certain extent depend on personal style. As you read through the following three chapters, first seek to understand how each idea could impact you and your team, and then decide what level of implementation may be appropriate, given your starting point, authority and aspirations.

FAST TRACK TOP TEN

This chapter presents a framework of methods or techniques to improve financial performance, understand finance, read annual reports, carry out investment appraisals, understand how your team and company is performing and make use of spreadsheets – all designed to make life as a team easier. Each function can take a lifetime to master, but the Fast Track manager will know which areas to focus on – get those areas right and the team will perform. Often success relates to the introduction of simple tools and techniques to improve effectiveness and efficiency.

Introducing finance tools and techniques

What needs to be included? – the top ten tools and techniques

We can divide the financial tools and techniques that a Fast Track team leader needs into two kinds:

→ **External.** Tools that deal with financial information about an organisation which they or other parties have published.

→ **Internal.** Techniques that make sure that the financial element of the business is assisting with the effectiveness and efficiency of a company as it generates profits and grows.

External tools

Depending where your interest lies, the published information you can read in hard copy or on company websites can be of enormous assistance. Investors use the information to help them decide which shares to buy, sell or hold on to. Fast Track managers seek information about their own companies, their customers' companies and their suppliers' companies. In all cases, the regular reading of the financial pages of a newspaper or magazine is the starting point:

1 **Analysing company strategy** is a quick method of using the financial pages and the annual report to work out what a company is trying to achieve.

On a regular basis the board and finance department of an enterprise reports to the shareholders on progress during the preceding period. They may issue reports at the half-year stage or even on a quarterly basis, but the biggest interest and publicity is given to the annual report. At the heart of this annual report are the audited figures describing the company's recent performance and the current state of its finances:

2 **The income statement**, often referred to as the profit and loss account, describes the operating performance of the company over the last year.

3 **The balance sheet** shows how well or badly the company is set up financially to face the challenges of the future.

4 **The cash flow statement** shows how cash flowed into and out of the company and how well set up the company is in cash terms to fund its strategy for the future.

5 **The five-year results** allow you to look at the long-term trends of the company's progress.

Internal tools

At any point in time the board of directors of a company is presented with a whole raft of projects that their managers and team wish to carry out. These projects should all fit well with the strategy the board is pursuing; so the problem is – which ones should be preferred and funded? The first thing is to make sure that the data each project presents is as accurate as possible: a statement of what will happen if the project is approved. Then the project can be translated into financial terms.

One particular financial tool comes in very handy here. It allows the board an objective analysis of the likely financial impact that each of the projects will have on the business. It even allows for very different types of project and timescales of implementation, boiling the financial impact down to a small number of figures that are truly comparable – 'apples with apples':

6 **Investment appraisal** is a technique for gathering the data to compare two or more projects.

Having gathered the data and weighed it up for risk, it is time to move to the mathematics of financial analysis:

7 **Financial analysis payback method and net present value** involves two quick and reasonably easy methods of financial appraisal. Net present value is the more complex method of the two, doing the financial comparison which takes timing, costs and benefits into account to boil the financial case down to a single comparable number: the net present value or NPV.

CASE STORY TELECOMS COMPANY, JR AND IAN'S STORY

Narrators JR is the operations director and Ian the sales director of a subsidiary of a global telecommunications operator.

Context The company was growing fast and was investing in equipment to meet the needs of customers and prospects. This was stretching its financial resources.

Issue There was always an argument when Ian, in sales, wanted to expand the equipment to satisfy a key customer. JR, in operations, charged the whole cost of the equipment to that deal and showed that Ian would make a loss. Ian argued that he would sell the same solution to other people and make further use of the asset. He could not at that time give an accurate estimate of how much more he would sell.

Solution The financial controller showed them how to create a cash flow with the cash outlay for equipment happening at the beginning of the project. With that cash flow, it was easy to work out what value Ian would have to

HP

sell to make the equipment break even. Ian then had to make a decision whether to accept that sales value as a key performance indicator or to reject the deal until he had sold the solution to other organisations. In the end there was, of course, a sensible compromise. Ian accepted a target for the year that would not quite cover the expenditure, but agreed to accept a higher target in that area the following year.

Learning When evaluating investment decisions, test the validity of estimates, particularly of benefits, by turning them into KPIs.

Every team leader gets regular financial information showing them what the company has recorded as their revenue from internal or external customers and what they spent during the same period. The expectation of managers in most cases is that the team's financial performance will show a profit. (The exceptions are teams charged with operating within a cost budget with no income stream and therefore no expectation of making profits.) Here we can use a financial analysis tool that helps managers plan and control their financial performance:

8 Breakeven analysis enables you to work out how much income you need to meet the 'fixed' costs of your profit centre. These costs occur regardless of whether you sell anything; generally the biggest of these is the bill for staff.

Now we move to the side of finance that is concerned with managing the business – budgetary control, an important and sometimes controversial tool:

9 Budgetary control.
The main mechanism by which senior managers measure the performance of their divisions and teams is known by a number of names – targets, budgets and so on. The most helpful term is key performance indicators:

10 Key performance indicators.

So, let's take a detailed look at these top ten techniques.

1 ANALYSING COMPANY STRATEGY

Let's start from how a management team, the board of directors or divisional managers plan their strategy. Strategy is probably the most misunderstood term in the business lexicon. When teams are trying to work out what their role is in contributing to the overall company strategy they take as long trying to decide what a strategy is as they do working out what it should be. So keep it really simple – a strategy defines what we are going to sell, to whom we are going to sell it and how we are going to do that.

What the planners of a business do is look at the current product set and then at the current markets in which they sell. The current product set is probably numerically huge and the markets they sell to quite complicated. So, they put the products into sensible product groups and the markets into groups or segments.

They may, for example, group their products by complexity of after-sales support; by value, so they can choose to emphasise high-value products; or by maturity, separating new products from well-established ones. In terms of markets, they may choose to do this simply by geography or by size of the customers' operations – for example, putting very large companies in the UK into a different set from small companies in the rest of Europe.

However they do this grouping, you can detect from the company's annual report what the groups are and where they are currently putting emphasis. The information is in the reports of the chairman and the directors. If you are studying a company in some detail you may want to document what you find in the form of a product/market matrix:

	MARKET A	MARKET B	MARKET C
Product set 1	H>L	M>L	L>H
Product set 2	M>H	0>M	0>M

The first letter in each box shows the current strategic emphasis, while the second letter shows the future strategic emphasis:

H = High level of activity using many resources

M = Medium level of activity

L = Low level of activity

0 = No activity at all

> = Change of emphasis from now into the future

From this example you can see that the company plans to take product set 2 into two totally new markets, while in most cases reducing the amount of activity put into product set 1. You need to keep this matrix up to date by watching for changes in the company. You can get this information from the business pages in a newspaper and from any contacts you have within the company.

The benefits of understanding a company's strategy can be considerable. A salesperson, for example, probably wants to be involved with parts of the company that are growing as opposed to parts where activity and therefore their importance to the board is diminishing. If you are in the purchasing department, studying the strategy of a supplier allows you to detect when a product that you buy from them is becoming less important to them.

Finally, if you are not sure about the strategy of the company you work for, this exercise will help to plug that gap and show whether you are operating in a part of the business that remains an important part of the strategy.

2 THE INCOME STATEMENT

Most managers are familiar with the concept of the profit and loss account, or income statement as it is now known. Indeed, most people understand the concept of comparing what you are earning with what you are spending. Let's explain the document and comment on each of the items, before showing some examples of how you can put them to use.

The income statement covers a period of time. Most large companies publish this statement twice a year. During the third quarter of the year they publish an income statement that covers the first half of the year, including comparisons with the first half of last year. During the first quarter of the next year they publish the full year's figures.

The income statement compares the sales revenue earned during a period with the costs incurred in making those sales. The figures are based on the accruals concept. That is, revenue is included for all goods dispatched, whether or not payment has been received by the end of the period. Similarly, cost will include the cost of all goods and services received before the end of the period. They may not have been paid for, or even invoiced, at the balance sheet date, but their cost is still included.

Here is an outline of the statement together with some explanation. Remember that there is always the glossary at the back of this book with more detailed definitions of financial jargon, and there is also an example of a full income statement on page 167 in the Director's Toolkit.

Revenue (or sales or turnover)
- Cost of sales
= Gross profit
+ Other income
- Distribution expenses
- Administrative expenses
- Other operating expenses
= Operating profit
+ Finance income
- Finance costs
= Profit before taxation
- Taxation
= **Profit for the year**

The top line of the income statement is the **revenue**, the sum of sales made. Outside the strict nomenclature of the formal income statement, people still refer to this as sales or turnover. Be careful, because turnover has a different meaning in the USA, where it is normally reserved for staff turnover.

From this we deduct the actual costs of the products sold. In the simple case of a bookshop, it is what the shop paid to purchase the books that have now been sold. In a manufacturing company, it includes all the direct costs of producing the products sold. The jargon used is **cost of sales**. A lot of managers also call these costs direct costs.

This gives us the **gross profit**. From the gross profit we can calculate the gross margin. This is a vital piece of information for monitoring purposes. How we run the business is dictated to a considerable extent by how big our gross margins are.

In fact, one of the most important characteristics of a business is its gross margin, or rather gross margins, since most companies sell a range of products and services that will probably have different margins. The gross margin of a product is the gross profit expressed as a percentage of the sales price.

So, if a product costs £100 to purchase from a supplier and the sales price is £125, the gross margin is 20%, calculated by 25/125. If a manufacturer has direct costs of manufacture of £1,000 for a product and the sales price, governed by market forces, is £1,600, the gross margin is 37.5%, calculated by 600/1,600.

In most cases there is a good reason for the margins that companies can achieve. For example, if there is a high level of after-sales support required then plainly the gross margin will have to be high. The costs of after-sales service and support come out of the gross profit.

Do you operate in a high or low gross margin business, or do different products have different margins? Computer companies provide some good examples of high and low margins in their product range. They might sell:

→ computer solutions, with hardware, packaged software and tailored software solutions;

→ computer systems;

→ commodities and consumables such as printers and printer toner.

Consider the gross margin of these product areas:

→ Computer solutions have a high gross margin. There is a lot of value added to the hardware by the software and consultancy that goes into building a solution. There may be a lot of support required to ensure customer satisfaction and that will be built into the quoted price. Remember, competitors have to do the same.

→ At a medium level are computer systems. Competitive pressures will tend to keep prices down, and in any case there is much less value added to the hardware and much of it will be a commodity mainly trading on price.

→ The lowest margins come in commodities and consumables, where fierce competition puts heavy pressure on selling prices.

When any businessperson looks at the characteristics of a business, the gross margin is an important starting point and allows them to make a good comparison between different industries. For example, think about two totally different industries – a company selling commercial aircraft and a package holiday company. As you would expect, the holiday company operates on very low margins – you can have an all-inclusive holiday for a week in Barbados for £500 – while the commercial aircraft manufacturer is exactly the opposite, with very high gross margins.

QUICK TIP *MOVE SLOWLY*

If you work in a low gross margin business, be careful not to make too many changes at the same time. You need to be able to see the exact impact on the income statement of any change. For example, if you change the copy of a marketing promotion, look at the end of the next quarter to see whether it has improved sales and profits.

From the gross margin we deduct the expenses. For annual reporting purposes they are usually divided into **distribution expenses**, **administrative expenses** and **other operating expenses**. It is fairly straightforward to know which is which. The costs of most of head office, for example, will go into administrative expenses, while the costs of running the fleet of delivery vans will be part of distribution expenses. In some businesses this is a crucial distinction, and some of the ratios in this area will be significant, but normally it is less important to distinguish between them. Management accounts prepared for internal purposes have more detail.

This gives us the **operating profit**. People often refer to this as earnings before interest and tax, or EBIT.

Now increase this by **finance income**, which is the interest the company has earned on cash balances, deposits and so on, and reduce it by **finance costs**, which is the interest it has paid on its loans and overdrafts, and you get the **profit before taxation**. There is no golden rule, but profit before taxation is generally the figure that people talk about when they are making comparisons. Business papers that say 'the profits are down' are probably referring to this number on the profit and loss account.

In addition to **profit for the year**, the other number you hear almost as often is **earnings per share**. This is the amount of profit for the year the company made per share available on the market. Earnings per share is shown at the bottom of the income statement, after profit for the year. The calculation for earnings per share is relatively simple: you take the number of outstanding shares (which you can find on the balance sheet or in the notes to the accounts) and divide it into the profit for the year (which you find on the income statement).

Basically, earnings per share show you how much money each shareholder made for each of their shares. In reality, this money does not get paid back to the shareholder. Instead, most is reinvested in future operations of the company. The profit for the year that is not distributed to shareholders in dividends is added to the retained earnings number on the balance sheet.

At the bottom of an income statement, you see two numbers:

→ **The basic earnings per share**. This is a calculation based on the number of shares outstanding at the time the income statement was developed.

→ **The diluted earnings per share**. This includes other potential shares that could eventually be outstanding. This category includes shares designated for things like share options or warrants (financial instruments that give the holder a right to buy shares at a set price, usually below the share's market value) and convertibles (shares promised to a holder of bonds or preference shares that are convertible to ordinary shares).

These numbers give you an idea of how much the company earned per share. You can use them to analyse the profitability of a company, which is explained in T2 Financial Ratio Analysis starting at page 167.

Dividends declared per share are sometimes shown at the foot of the income statement under the earnings per share information. Otherwise, this detail will be in the notes to the accounts. The company's board of directors may declare dividends quarterly, biannually or annually.

A useful ratio that you can calculate from the income statement is the return on sales. This is profit before taxation divided by revenues. You can compare the profitability of one company with another using this ratio, as well as the trends in one company from last year to this.

3 THE BALANCE SHEET

The balance sheet is a more difficult concept for most people to understand than the income statement, but the two statements together give much better clues to the health and prospects of a company than the income statement on its own. Indeed, at the top of a business much more emphasis is placed on understanding the impact of events on the balance sheet, while middle managers are more concerned with the shorter-term profit position.

One of the differences between the two documents is that an income statement shows what happened over a period of time, while a balance sheet is a snapshot of the company's position at a moment in time. This moment could be any day in the financial year, but the one we are most familiar with is the balance sheet produced at the end of the company's financial year and published with the annual report.

The headings used in a balance sheet are:

Non-current assets
+ Current assets
= Total assets

Current liabilities
+ Non-current liabilities
= Total liabilities

Net assets (= Total assets – Total liabilities)

Equity

The amount shown as the net assets in the balance sheet will always equal the amount shown for equity. Perhaps the simplest explanation for this is to say that accountancy is based on the principles of double-entry bookkeeping. The term double entry refers to the fact that every transaction undertaken by a business will be recorded in the books twice – once as a debit and once as a credit. Therefore, if, at any time, all the debit entries in the books are totalled then their sum will be exactly the same as the total of all the credit entries. This is known as a trial balance. A balance sheet is simply a trial balance that has been organised in such a way as to provide useful information to the reader.

What the company owns is called **assets** and what the business owes is called **liabilities**.

We group the assets by time considerations. **Non-current assets** are those that will give benefit to the company over a term that is longer than one year. Many people still call these fixed assets. The non-current assets are subdivided into tangible and intangible.

Tangible non-current assets include property – the offices, shops or factories that the company uses in its day-to-day activities. They also include plant and equipment, which includes motor vehicles and the fittings of offices, shops and factories. For example, think of a situation where a company buys a fleet of vans to distribute its products around the country. The company will use those vans for a minimum of three years and maybe a good bit longer. It does not seem right, therefore, to charge as a cost to the income statement the full value of the vans at the time they were bought; it seems more sensible to charge for them over their useful life, say a third of the cost price per year for three years. This process is called the depreciation of tangible assets. Non-current assets are shown on the balance sheet after deducting accumulated depreciation.

Land and property can be different, since, in the long term, they are liable to appreciate in value. A company may record that appreciation from time to time based on an independent valuation. Despite this, they still charge depreciation on land and property like any other asset.

Intangible assets are becoming less common on balance sheets. There is a healthy suspicion of assets that are said to have a value but no substance. There is probably one exception to this and that is goodwill, which you will certainly see on many balance sheets where companies have bought up other companies. Goodwill arises when the amount paid for a company exceeds, as it normally does, the value of the assets in the purchased company. When the buying company absorbs these assets on to its balance sheet, therefore, liabilities will rise higher than assets. For this reason you 'balance' the accounts by showing that you have purchased the asset of goodwill. This goodwill is an intangible asset, such as a loyal customer base or a popular product range.

Non-current assets also include the long-term investments the company holds, such as investment property, investments in joint ventures and associate companies, and investments in other companies that the board expects to be holding for the long term, often referred to as trade investments.

Current assets are those that the company is likely to turn into cash within the next 12 months:

→ **Inventories**. These are often referred to as 'stock', are the stock of finished goods not yet sold or delivered. A manufacturer also includes work in progress and raw materials in its stock.

→ **Trade and other receivables**. These are are mainly the amounts that customers owe for unpaid invoices.

→ **Cash and cash equivalents**. These are are the most liquid asset of all.

Now let's turn to liabilities, where once again the same distinction occurs, with non-current and current liabilities.

Current liabilities are those liabilities that the company will have to pay within the next 12 months. It is a strict definition; in fact balance sheets used to use the expression 'Creditors – amounts falling due within one year'.

In this category we include the following:

→ **Trade and other payables**. These are debts that the company has that must be paid over the next 12 months. They include trade creditors, which is the money owed to suppliers.

→ **Borrowings and other financial liabilities**. These are the amounts owed to banks – for example, overdrafts used in current accounts to cover the short-term fluctuations of money going out and money coming in. There are many and varied ways of raising short-term finance, all of which are included here.

→ **Current tax liabilities**. This is tax due to be paid in the next 12 months.

→ **Provisions**. These are amounts that may or may not become payable but which it is prudent to include in the balance sheet. An example of this could be money that is being disputed in an argument about a contract. The finance director will provision the amount if it is considered more likely than not that the dispute will be settled in the creditor's favour.

→ **Other current liabilities**. These any remaining items. You can see the details of these in the notes to the accounts.

So much for current liabilities. **Non-current liabilities** are sometimes referred to as fixed liabilities. In the balance sheet, non-current liabilities only include external liabilities. Liabilities to the shareholders are included under the heading **equity**.

External liabilities include the following:

→ **Borrowings and other financial liabilities**. These are the long-term debts owed to banks and other institutions. The detail is available in the notes to the accounts.

→ **Deficits on pension schemes**. These occur when the company has an obligation to fund a pension scheme. Note that if the pension scheme is in surplus it would then appear as a non-current asset in the balance sheet.

→ **Deferred tax liabilities**. These arise because accounts deal with some items differently from the way they are dealt with for tax purposes.

→ **Provisions**. These have been explained above under current liabilities. Provisions can also be non-current liabilities where it is expected that any payment will be made after more than one year.

Equity will include shareholders' equity and minority interests. Shareholders' equity (previously known as shareholders' funds) normally includes the following elements:

→ **Share capital**. This is the nominal value of the issued shares. In the case of most UK shares, they are valued at a nominal 25 pence each and in the USA at one dollar. In fact, this nominal value, or par value, has little practical importance. What is more important is the total proceeds of a share issue.

→ **Share premium account**. This arises when the company sells shares not at par value but somewhere near the current market value. The difference between those numbers is recorded in the share premium account.

→ **Reserves**. These include the profits that the company has retained over the years. The bottom line of the income statement – profit for the year – less any dividends paid is added to last year's number to give the new value of reserves or retained earnings. Companies that have been trading for a long time will have a lot of money in reserves. There are some other types of reserves, such as the revaluation reserve, which arises when assets are revalued.

→ **Minority interests**. These are similar to reserves. They record what part of the group reserves belongs to minority interests. Profits that have been made by companies within the group which have other shareholders (apart from the parent company which is presenting the report) will belong partly to those other shareholders.

Once again, the terminology will change according to the situation and the norms agreed by the finance director. You can see the detail contained in a full report by studying the balance sheet on page 168.

From the balance sheet we can calculate a number of useful ratios. For example, we can calculate gearing. This compares shareholders' funds with the amount that the company has borrowed from outsiders. Companies with high levels of debt are riskier in the sense that they will need to meet their commitment to pay interest before there is any money left over to pay dividends or finance growth. On the other hand, companies with high gearing can use the borrowed money to invest in more projects and hence achieve faster growth. In good times this will give shareholders better returns, but in bad times the companies will end up in liquidation. We have rarely had a better example of this than the banking crisis of 2008.

4 THE CASH FLOW STATEMENT

Cash is a company's life-blood. If a company expects to manage its assets and liabilities and to pay its obligations, it has to know the amount of cash flowing into and out of the business. This is not always easy to work out when using accrual accounting, where amounts are recognised in the income statement in the period in which the transaction occurred, which is not necessarily the same as the period in which cash was received or paid.

Accrual accounting makes it very hard to work out how much cash a company actually holds, because cash does not have to change hands for a company to record a transaction. The statement of cash flows is the financial statement that helps the financial report reader understand a company's cash position by adjusting for differences between cash and accruals. This statement tracks the cash that flows in and out of a business during a specified period of time, and lays out the sources of that cash. Here is an outline of the cash flow statement (there is a detailed example on page 169 in the Director's Toolkit):

Cash flows from operating activities
    Items of inflow
      − Items of outflow
  = Cash generated from operations
      − Interest paid
      − Taxation paid
  = Net cash from operating activities

Cash flows from investing activities
    Items of inflow
      − Items of outflow
  = Net cash from investing activities

Cash flows from financing activities

    Items of inflow

    – Items of outflow

= Net cash used in financing activities

Net cash inflow/(outflow) from activities

Net cash and cash equivalents at beginning of the year

Net cash and cash equivalents at end of the year

As you can see, there are three distinct parts of the statement:

→ **Operating activities.** These include cash that was taken into the company through sales of its products or services, as well as cash that was paid out to suppliers and employees. This section also includes the tax payable on operating activities as an outflow. This method of presentation is known as the direct method and is encouraged by accounting standards because it is easy to understand. The alternative method (the indirect method), which you may come across, starts with the profit before tax and then adjusts this figure to remove non-cash items such as depreciation. When using the indirect method, it is also necessary to adjust for movements in working capital, since profit is based on the accruals concept and the cash flow statement must be constructed on a pure cash basis.

→ **Investing activities.** These include the purchase or sale of the company's investments, which can include the purchase or sale of long-term assets, such as a building or a company division. Spending on capital improvements (upgrades to assets held by the company, such as the renovation of a building) also fits in this category, as does any buying or selling of short-term investments. This section also includes any income received from investments.

→ **Financing activities.** These involve raising cash through long-term debt or by issuing new shares. This section also includes using cash to pay down debt or buy back shares. Companies also include any dividends paid here.

Net cash inflow/(outflow) from activities is the total of the three parts. This is then added to the cash situation at the start of the year to give the net cash of the company at the end of the period.

The usefulness of the statement of cash flow comes in answering three questions:

→ Where did the company get the cash needed for operations during the period shown on the statement – from revenue generated, funds borrowed or issue of new shares?

→ What cash did the company actually spend during the periods shown on the statement?

→ What was the change in the cash balance during each of the years shown on the statement? Remember that the statement shows the previous year as well as last year.

Knowing the answers to these questions helps you determine whether the company is thriving and has the cash needed to continue and to grow its operations, or whether it appears to have a cash flow problem and could be nearing a point of disaster.

Now you need to combine two of the essential top ten tools to get a further insight into the company. Remind yourself of what you learnt about the company when you used the first tool and analysed the strategy of the company. Compare this with what the cash flow statement tells you, and you should be able to detect how well the cash situation supports the strategy. If, for example, the company strategy includes rapid growth by acquisition, then it will need a strong cash performance to make this possible.

QUICK TIP MISSION STATEMENTS
Be careful with mission statements; often they are no more than a long slogan and reveal little about the company's strategy. If this is the case, look at the chairman's statement to find a longer version of the company's objectives.

If the strategy is for strong organic growth within the existing business but its inventories are growing faster than sales, then there may be a misfit between the strategy and the cash situation. If the chairman's statement concentrates on customer service but accounts receivable are going up more pro rata than sales, then there could be more customer dissatisfaction rather than less – you need to know what is going on in the real world as opposed to the world of directors' reports.

5 THE FIVE-YEAR RESULTS

Most companies include in their annual report figures for the last five years and then produce some ratios from them so that readers can see the trends in performance. The good thing about this is that the ratios are calculated for you. The problem is that the directors can choose what ratios to publish and how to calculate them. Generally speaking, it is better to calculate your own ratios. That way you can take an independent view of the company's performance, and since you are using the same ratios for all companies you are reviewing, you will have a basis for comparing like with like. How to do this is explained in T2 Financial Ratio Analysis starting at page 167.

Here is an example of a five-year summary published in an annual report:

YEARS ENDED 31 DECEMBER		2008	2007	2006	2005	2004
Gross margin	Gross profit/ Revenue	**35.8%**	38.7%	38.3%	36.7%	35.3%
Net margin	Operating profit/ Revenue	**11.4%**	12.2%	10.5%	8.7%	9.1%
Profitability	Profit before tax/ Revenue	**10.5%**	10.8%	9.8%	8.7%	9.4%
Dividend per share declared in respect of the year		**20.5p**	18.3p	16.0p	13.1p	11.5p
Dividend cover	Profit attributable to shareholders/ Dividend payable	**2.0×**	2.4×	2.2×	2.9×	2.8×
Return on equity	Profit attributable to shareholders/ Average equity shareholders' funds	**40.6%**	44.8%	45.0%	35.1%	35.2%

You might interpret these figures as follows:

→ **There was a steady improvement in gross margins for the first four years**. This seems to have been reversed in 2008. It may be that the company is having to reduce its selling prices because of the difficult economic conditions in 2008.

→ **The company seems to have worked hard to limit the impact of the reduced gross margin, since the net margin and the profitability ratio are not much lower than they were in 2007**. This may indicate excessive cost cutting, which could be effective in the short term but may leave the company unable to respond to an upturn in the economy because of a lack of resources.

→ **Despite the problems, dividends have continued to increase at a rapid rate**. This probably means that the directors are trying to reassure the shareholders that the company is still on target to achieve its long-term goals.

6 INVESTMENT APPRAISAL

Reading the income statement, balance sheet and cash flow statement gives you a good idea of the history of a company's performance. The management accounting system is useful for telling managers how their performance is at the moment. It is now time to turn to a tool that combines management skills with financial techniques to predict the future. Managers need to get into a position where they can convert estimates for business success into a convincing story of why one project or way of investing the company's money should be preferred over another.

Most business decisions are made on calculated assessments by experienced people of what will occur if the business takes a certain course of action. The financial technique is a great tool to aid decision making, but a decision-making tool should never be mistaken for the decision itself.

For example, a sales manager is discussing with one of her account managers the possibility of his taking on another salesperson. The account manager is keen to get the extra resource, since he knows that there is more business in his account if he could cover the ground more effectively. The manager is happy to find the money for the new person but has to be convinced that she is putting her scarce resources into the most productive area. So, the answer to her first question 'Will you sell more if we put another salesperson on your patch?' is easy: 'Sure we will.' The second question is much more difficult: 'How much more?'

Now consider what is going through the account manager's mind. He knows that if he claims a very high figure, say £5 million, his manager may be sceptical but will probably be sufficiently impressed to let him have the resource. But at what cost? She will, of course, change the estimate into a management objective, and the account manager's target will go up by £5 million or an amount that recognises that it will take a while to get the new person up to speed. If, on the other hand, the account manager goes low, saying 'Well, for the first year I think we must allow a settling-in period and maybe expect £100,000', there are probably other account managers who will offer the sales manager a better deal than this and she will prefer to give them the resource. So he has to go somewhere between these two. He wants to be successful and to be seen to be successful. This means that he would rather take a target of £900,000 and make £950,000 than take a target of £1 million and get £950,000. The first is success; the second is failure. And so his thoughts go on. He will try to agree a number that he really believes he can achieve but that will be attractive enough to get his boss's agreement to the hiring of the person.

This may seem slightly cynical and to lack some logic, but actually if everyone is competent at their jobs it can work quite well. An experienced sales manager will probably be able to give a reasonable estimate of what their resources will bring in. It is, after all, one of the things they are there for.

This example is typical of the way managers set parameters for decision making, and how they discuss and arrive at decisions, particularly in big companies. Middle managers are encouraged to have ideas, to estimate the benefits of the idea and convince their managers that they should be allowed to go ahead. Most are circumspect and cautious about their claims, but some do have a rush of blood to the head and claim huge, but unbelievable, results for their pet project. To deal with both the optimist and the pessimist, organisations need a process that examines ideas dispassionately. This is called the investment appraisal system.

Introduction to investment appraisal

We have noticed that when you are a manager and a member of your team asks to see you, as opposed to you asking to see them, they are almost certainly going to bid for resources to carry out some new activities and improve profits.

The creation of a business case template is a good start to the investment appraisal process. It helps people to know what management is looking for and ensures that new ideas conform with the company's overall strategy. But strategic thinking is only the first part of the system. The rest of the process involves the following steps:

→ choose a timescale

→ estimate the benefits

→ estimate the costs

→ produce a projected profit and loss account.

We will take these steps one at a time as we examine how companies decide to invest their resources.

Choose a timescale

Most investment opportunities need in the first place a combination of capital expenditure, which is mainly on fixed assets, and revenue expenditure, which is money to finance the people and other running costs. Fixed assets have a depreciation period agreed by the finance people to be a reasonable estimate of the productive life of the asset. This depreciation period is frequently the timescale chosen to measure the viability of a project involving capital expenditure, where, for example, the company needs to invest in refurbishing a retail outlet.

Another element in the decision on timescales is the length of time it takes for the project to get started. It would be less than useful to measure the benefit of a construction project – for example, a tunnel between England and France – without taking into account that the period from inception to operation will be more than ten years. For the finances to work in such a project, its revenue earning life will need to be extended to perhaps 50 years.

Timescales for investment appraisal should be sensible. They should reflect the real life of the project, and if it is known at the start that further investment will be required during the time chosen, then that expenditure should be added into the equation.

Estimate the benefits

This is perhaps the most difficult part of the estimating process. As we have seen, there is often an emotional overtone for managers who are making the estimates, as they are aware that there will be increased targets or stiffer objectives if the expenditure is approved. It is useful for estimating reasons to break down the benefits into four categories:

→ increases in revenue

→ reduction in costs

→ avoidance of future costs

→ improvements in control.

Let's take these one at a time.

Increases in revenue

The top line of any proposed profit and loss account is sales. This is true whether the sales are external (to the company's customers) or internal (to other departments within the business). Expenditure of money will often have as the first part of the justification claims that revenues will increase.

Usually when estimating revenues you will need to use a range of results.

The most common method of doing this is to consider three possibilities:

→ **Pessimistic:** the lowest outcome that you believe possible.

→ **Most likely:** your view of what will actually happen.

→ **Optimistic:** the best, but still feasible, outcome.

Here is an example of an IT manager estimating the revenue stream from a new system that she is going to try to sell to various divisions in the company. She divides them into three categories defined by the likelihood that they will come on board and purchase the system. This will be the basis for the projected profit and loss account she needs to raise to start the business case. The pessimistic case assumes that only the prospects in likelihood 1 will place an order. The most likely case adds the prospects in likelihood 2, and the optimistic assumes all the prospects will agree:

YEAR	1	2	3
Pessimistic (likelihood 1)	465.3	814.8	814.8
Most likely (likelihood 1 + 2)	666.6	1,099.2	1,099.2
Optimistic (likelihood 1 + 2 + 3)	792.6	1,267.2	1,267.2

Reduction in costs

When assessing a spending project this area is likely to be very important. Finance people are likely to agree that a reduction of costs is the most tangible benefit there is. However, you have to make sure that the costs claimed as a reduction are relevant costs. If, for example, someone can do with less office space, that only becomes a reduction in cost if the company can stop paying rent on the office or move someone else in.

As you try to make a business case the aim is to find sufficient benefits to justify the expense. Most importantly, a manager who will have to take a drop in expenditure budget – since that is how the cost reduction will be realised – must agree to any reduction in cost. As we saw with increases in sales, many managers respond very cautiously to an argument that they can do with a smaller budget. In the end, business cases are well made when reductions in costs outweigh the expenses of the project. Other benefits will make a reasonable case into a good one.

Remember that estimates are not facts; they are negotiable. The agreement of a manager to a small percentage saving in a large cost can have a dramatic effect on the business case.

Avoidance of future costs

The avoidance of future costs is a slightly different concept from a straightforward reduction in costs. This brings into the business case any costs that would be incurred if the project were not undertaken. If, for example, a company decides to refurbish a retail outlet, it will avoid the costs of the normal routine repairs and maintenance that would be necessary to keep the current fittings up to standard.

Improvements in control

Companies are continuously re-engineering their business processes. If they change their strategy in any way or react to changes in technology, they will almost certainly have to review some of their business processes. This almost always ends up with capital and revenue expenditure and is often justified by the fact that it affords management better control over the business. This may be good enough for the people running the business, but it is not sufficiently concrete for the finance department. They want to know how this benefit will turn into cash.

Improvements in control can be difficult to quantify, but if you do not do so then the finance people will not let you put them in the business case. The way to do this normally involves a manager agreeing to take a more stretching target for the next period because of the extra control. A production manager may agree to accept a higher productivity target if they fit expensive instruments to give better information on the current state of their machinery.

Estimate the costs

In comparison with benefits, costs are more straightforward to estimate. You will find they fall into the categories of staff, equipment rental, depreciation of purchased assets, facilities and consumables. It is always better to agree costs with a supplier, since this removes any risk that they might be wrong. Once again, make sure that the costs are relevant.

Produce a projected profit and loss account

Going back to the example of the IT manager, she now lists the costs carefully, having agreed to take a three-year timescale for the project. This is the projected profit and loss account for the project:

YEAR	1	2	3
Expenditure			
Staff	70.0	70.0	70.0
Maintenance	0.0	35.0	35.0
Depreciation	485.0	485.0	486.0
Accommodation	18.0	18.0	18.0
Electricity	15.0	15.0	15.0
Sundries	43.0	43.0	43.0
Total	631.0	666.0	667.0
Income (see p. 64)	666.6	1,099.2	1,099.2
Profit	35.6	433.2	432.2

This looks like a reasonable business case, but we need to compare this project with others the company could do. Two techniques are involved in this – risk analysis and net present value. We deal with risk analysis in the Director's Toolkit on page 179 and net present value in the next top ten tool.

QUICK TIP *A PROBLEM IS NOT NECESSARILY A DEAL BREAKER*
When your plan tells you that a particular event could scupper a project's financial feasibility, treat it as an opportunity to work on avoiding that event rather than a threat to the implementation of the entire project.

7 FINANCIAL ANALYSIS Payback method and net present value

It is quite possible for a company to be making profits but be failing for lack of cash. The major reason for this is that the profit and loss account will show the cost of fixed assets being spread over a period of time by depreciation, whereas when a company buys a fixed asset the cash has to be paid out immediately. For this reason companies will always look at cash flow forecasts as well as the projected profit and loss account when considering the future. Similarly, when we appraise an individual project we need to consider the effect on both cash and profit.

Before we consider the main method used by most businesspeople to calculate return on investment – net present value – let's take a quick look at the other method commonly used.

Payback method

This method measures the length of time from the first payment of cash until the total receipts of cash from the investment equals the total payment made on that investment. It does not in any way attempt to measure the profitability of the project, and it restricts all calculations to a receipts and payments basis.

When considering alternative projects, the one with the shortest payback period is the one that is preferred:

	PROJECT 1	PROJECT 2
Asset cost	10,000	15,000
Net cash flow:		
Year 1	2,000	3,000
Year 2	3,000	4,000
Year 3	3,000	6,000
Year 4	4,000	8,000
Year 5	10,000	2,000
Payback period	3.5 years	3.25 years

In this case the second project would be preferred, despite the fact that the positive cash flow for project 1 ramps up in the fifth year.

The payback method has the advantage of being quick and simple, but it has two major disadvantages as well:

→ It considers only cash received during the payback period and ignores anything received afterwards.

→ It does not take into account the dates on which the cash is actually received. So, it is possible to have two projects both costing the same, with the same payback period, but with different cash flows.

In the next example, the two projects have the same payback period. However, it is obvious that, without any further information, we should prefer project 2, since the cash is received earlier and can therefore be reinvested in another project to earn more profits:

	PROJECT 1	PROJECT 2
Asset cost	10,000	10,000
Net cash flow:		
Year 1	1,000	3,000
Year 2	3,000	3,000
Year 3	3,000	3,000
Year 4	3,000	1,000
Year 5	4,000	4,000
Payback period	4 years	4 years

It is in fact very difficult to know which of these projects is better for the business simply by using the payback method of investment appraisal. The fact that they both pay back in four years suggests that both projects are equally good. The second project gets a better return of £2,000 in the first year, which would probably make it the better investment, but you cannot really tell.

Despite its disadvantages, the payback method is still useful for quite complex projects. This is particularly true where there is a great deal of early capital investment in infrastructure, followed by a lengthy period of income derived from those assets.

Discounted cash flow

So, we need a method of investment appraisal that takes into account the timing of the cash flows as well as their absolute amount. Discounted cash flow does just that.

Suppose we offer to give you £1,000. Would you prefer to have it now or in five years' time? Obviously now, since if you want to spend the money it will be worth more now than it will be after five years of even modest inflation. But what if you don't need to spend it now? Then you still want the use of it so that you can put it somewhere it will earn money. You will therefore have more to spend in five years' time.

But, you have assumed that we are paying no interest in the five years. Suppose we say that if you take it in five years' time we will pay you 50% per annum compound interest. Now, of course, you would prefer to wait. In five years' time we will give you £7,593.75. Even if you needed to spend the money now, you could borrow it and still have a hefty profit in five years.

The concept of discounted cash flow is based on the usefulness of being able to calculate what interest percentage we would have to pay you for it to make no difference at all whether you take the money now or in five years. For the sake of argument, we know it is probably somewhere between 0 and 50%.

The mechanics of discounted cash flow

To arrive at a method of doing this, consider the following scenario:

You have inherited £10,000 from your godfather. Unfortunately, he had heard that you are liable to spend money fairly freely so he says that you cannot receive the cash until your 30th birthday. You are 27 today (happy birthday!).

Your godfather was actually fairly well informed. You are desperate to get this money before lunchtime tomorrow in order to place a bet on a horse someone has told you is going to do well in the 2.30 race. You have found a friendly banker who will advance you part of the £10,000.

The interest rate is 10% per annum and she is prepared to advance you an amount A, such that with interest you will owe the bank exactly £10,000 in three years' time. How much can you get?

→ If you borrow £100 now, you will owe interest of £10 by the end of one year, so the total outstanding will be £110.

→ During the second year, interest will be charged on the total amount outstanding of £110, i.e. interest of £11. The total outstanding would be £121.

→ During the third year, interest will be charged on the total amount outstanding of £121, i.e. interest of £12.10. The total outstanding would then be £133.10.

We can see, therefore, that for every £100 borrowed, £133.10 must be repaid at the end of the three-year period. Therefore the equation is:

$$A \times 1.331 = £10,000$$

The amount A will tell us how much you can borrow now, about £7,510, so that repayments of interest and capital will be £10,000.

This technique can of course be generalised to deal with any rate of interest and any time period.

We can now develop a method to compare two projects. Cash flows due in the future may be converted to equally desirable cash flows due today using the above method. This technique is known as discounting, and the equivalent cash flow due today is known as a present value.

TIMING OF CASH FLOW	AMOUNT OF CASH FLOW	DISCOUNT FACTOR AT 10%	PRESENT VALUE
Immediate	(10,000)	1.000	(10,000)
After 1 year	3,000	0.909	2,727
After 2 years	4,000	0.826	3,304
After 3 years	5,000	0.751	3,755
After 4 years	3,000	0.683	2,049
Net present value			1,835

Discount factors may be found from tables or by using the formula:

$$1/(1 + i)^n \text{ where } i = \text{discount rate and } n = \text{number of years}$$

Note that when we are calculating net present values, we refer to the interest rate of 10% as a discount rate to reflect the fact that we are now doing the calculations backwards!

In particular, consider the discount factor used above for year 3: 0.751. When deciding how much you could borrow from the bank in respect of your godfather's bequest, we divided £10,000 by 1.331. It is an exactly equivalent calculation to multiply £10,000 by 0.751 – the discount factor for three years at 10%. The final result takes into account all cash flows by totalling them and is known as the net present value (NPV) of the project.

If compelled to choose between two projects, we will select the one with the higher net present value. If we have a large number of projects, all of which can be undertaken, then we would wish to invest in every project with a positive net present value.

This would be a good time to check our assertion that NPV is a better technique than payback in distinguishing between projects. Consider the two projects we looked at earlier which had the same payback period of four years. We said then that project 2 should be preferred, since more money came in at the early stages of the project. Now let's calculate the NPV of each project:

	DISCOUNT FACTOR AT 10%	PROJECT 1	PRESENT VALUE	PROJECT 2	PRESENT VALUE
Asset cost	1.00	10,000	−10,000	10,000	−10,000
Net cash flow					
Year 1	0.909	1,000	909	3,000	2,727
Year 2	0.826	3,000	2,478	3,000	2,478
Year 3	0.751	3,000	2,253	3,000	2,253
Year 4	0.683	3,000	2,049	1,000	683
Year 5	0.621	4,000	2,484	4,000	2,484
NPV			173		625

Using discounted cash flows

Here are a few points to bear in mind when using discounted cash flows:

→ The initial investment occurs at time 0, the start of the project. Further cash flows then arise throughout the first year, but all these are combined to give one figure for the whole year.

→ Cash flows must be relevant costs and benefits.

→ The discount rate represents the cost of capital. In a large company the treasury function (the part of the finance department that looks after cash flow) will say what this should be.

→ Projects with a positive net present value add to the value of the company, so if they meet other business case template criteria, they should generally be accepted.

→ There is another numerical concept called the internal rate of return, or IRR. Remember the question, 'When would you like to be given £1,000?' We said that it was possible to work out an interest rate that would make it completely immaterial whether or not you took the money now or later. This is the IRR, the discount factor at which the NPV is reduced to zero. However, would you rather have 10% of £50 million, or 20% of £5 million? An easy question, since the first value is £5 million and the second £1 million; but if you make decisions based only on the IRR, you may well opt for the second. Always use the NPV for decision making.

→ If you work for a large company and are involved in investment appraisal, make sure that you know what its discount factor is. It may be the same as its notional cost of capital or it may be much higher. Some companies want technology projects to give a positive NPV when tested against a discount factor of 15% or greater.

8 BREAKEVEN ANALYSIS

Used correctly, this simple technique allows you to make the fine-tuning adjustments that help your team to go from a mediocre performance to a great one. The difference between success and failure in a new business revolves around how long it takes for the business to start making a profit. While it is still spending more money than it is receiving in sales revenues, its owners remain uncertain whether they have got a winner. So it is with a profit centre team, particularly a new team. It needs to be up and running and showing a profit as quickly as possible.

We will use a small business, a pub, to illustrate what breakeven analysis is and what its benefits are to your team. Every month a landlord spends money, regardless of whether anyone comes through the door to buy something. These expenses are called, quite reasonably, fixed costs. They include the rental of the premises, insurances, staff costs, maintenance work, marketing costs and so on. As part of their plan landlords need to make an absolutely complete list of these: if they miss anything out the calculation goes horribly wrong. You need to do the same for your team's fixed costs. The internal system may or may not give you such figures, but you have to make that list in any case.

Some businesses only have fixed costs. What this means is that no matter how much revenue comes in, they only have the fixed costs to cover before they reach the breakeven point. This gives them a very simple breakeven analysis. A transport business is a good example of this. If a bus company runs on a scheduled basis it uses the same amount of fuel and incurs all the other overheads whether its buses are full or half empty. The breakeven analysis is therefore quite straightforward. It is when the sum of the fares the customers have paid on each run make up the overheads of the run.

Other costs that companies incur are called variable costs and only occur when a customer buys something. They are the cost of the drink in the pub or the cost of buying the pen in the newsagent. The more you sell, the higher the variable costs. However, since you are selling the items for more than you paid for them, the contribution that the sale has made towards your fixed costs and subsequently your profits is also higher. People call it all sorts of things, but the word contribution is very appropriate: when you have worked out the difference between what customers paid for your products and what you paid for them, you have the contribution that the profit from that revenue has made to fixed costs.

QUICK TIP *KNOW YOUR COSTS*
Have a detailed knowledge of your fixed costs. There is probably nothing more important in running a business or a profit centre.

Here is the formula in equation form:

Revenues
– Direct costs
= Contribution
– Fixed costs
= Net profit

You will hear these terms and others to describe the same equation, but you can easily work out what the words mean if you fully understand the concept.

It should be easy enough to know the team's fixed costs. Don't fool yourself though; if some costs are slightly uncertain then take the higher end of the possibilities. It's crucial to start from an accurate estimate of these costs. If you guess too high, that's better than going the other way. You can always adjust the figure when you have real experience as the months go by.

The next bit is trickier. You have to make an estimate of the contribution that you will make when the customers, internal or external, start buying. This can be simple if you're selling a small number of easily identifiable products – an art gallery, for example, knows what it paid for each picture and therefore the profit it will make if it sells them for the price on the tag.

But it is not always so easy. Let's go back to our simple example to make the point. Suppose you were running a pub that sold only Guinness. From your supplier you would know exactly how much each pint that you sell has cost you. We're going to ignore VAT for the purposes of this exercise. Here's the equation where the selling price of a pint is £3 and you buy it in at £1:

→ The contribution for each pint is £3 – £1 = £2.

→ Your fixed costs are £1,200 per week; so you need to sell 600, i.e. 1,200 divided by 2, to cover the fixed costs.

→ 600 pints is therefore your breakeven point.

That way it's dead easy; but this Guinness-only scenario is unlikely because you will sell all sorts of other drinks too. But if you stick with drinks only, you should be able to estimate the average cost of all the drinks you sell. You can use that figure for planning purposes and adjust it with experience. For example, if your average drinks price for the whole range is £3.50, the average variable cost is £1.50 and your fixed costs have risen to £1,600 per week, then you need to sell £1,600 divided by £2 to find out the number of drinks you have to sell – 800, with a sales revenue of £2,800.

But, of course, you sell food as well, and the margin on food ingredients is very different from those on drinks. Again, you have to make an estimate. Using your common sense, you can work out a reasonable way of doing it. Perhaps you estimate the ratio of drinks to food that customers will consume. Say at lunchtime someone who spends £6 on food is likely to spend £5 on two drinks. In the evening many people will only drink, but a customer who spends £15 on food may well spend £12 on drinks. And so on.

However you do it, you now have an estimate of the contribution that sales make to fixed costs and profits. Say your best estimate is an overall contribution of 50%, because on average you sell the products for double the price you paid for them. And let's say your monthly fixed costs are £6,000. At what point does the contribution from sales equal the total of your fixed costs? That's your breakeven point.

You may need to do some snooping here and get your hands on the stock policies of some other pubs; you'll probably get these from your suppliers. This will show you the likely product mix. The mix varies quite significantly from pub to pub. Pubs with sport will have a much higher-percentage in beer, while a club will lean towards spirits. It's all based on common sense, but it needs a bit of imagination to gather data.

So here is the example in equation form:

Sales	12,000
Variable costs	6,000
Contribution	6,000
Fixed costs	6,000
Profit	0

If you do this on a spreadsheet you can play with the figures to your heart's content. You can try halving the sales and see how bad the situation could become. You could have another look at your fixed costs and see whether there are any economies there, and so on.

One situation that can catch people out is deciding which of the following options is better:

➜ to increase prices by 10%, when you know this will reduce sales quantity by 10%;

➜ to reduce prices by 10%, which will increase sales quantity by 10%.

Suppose the starting position is:

Sales	2,000 units at £6	12,000
Variable costs	2,000 units at £3	6,000
Contribution		6,000
Fixed costs		6,000
Profit		0

Increasing prices gives the following:

Sales	1,800 units at £6.60	11,880
Variable costs	1,800 units at £3	5,400
Contribution		6,480
Fixed costs		6,000
Profit		480

Reducing prices gives the following:

Sales	2,200 units at £5.40	11,880
Variable costs	2,200 units at £3	6,600
Contribution		5,280
Fixed costs		6,000
Loss		−720

So the decision to increase prices gives the better profit.

The term cost-volume-profit analysis is sometimes used to describe this extension of the breakeven technique.

9 BUDGETARY CONTROL

A budget is simply a plan. Strictly, a budget is a plan expressed in financial terms, but companies will, for example, produce budgets for material usage, manpower requirements and other resources as well as for accounting purposes. Indeed, budgets that overemphasise the financial side can give much less help to the managers of the business. This is why it is so useful to involve your team in developing your budget – they know what information they need and what critical factors to get right if they are to be successful.

The budgeting system or cycle tends to be an annual ritual. Divisions and departments are required to make detailed estimates of what they expect to earn and spend for the next year.

Budgets should achieve three objectives. They should:

→ assist in the planning process of the company;

→ help in coordinating the activities of the various parts of the organisation;

→ enable the company to control its operations.

The budgetary process should also be useful in forcing the team to examine closely its operation so that it can produce a viable budget.

The starting point will always be the sales budget. It is the sales budget that determines the level of materials and staff required, the production budget and machinery usage. From the sales budget we can determine costs and hence profit.

So how is a sales budget set? Three factors will be taken into account:

→ What is our past experience? What trends can we identify that may help us predict sales this year?

→ What is the current state of the market? What do the sales director and staff say about current prospects?

→ What sales level would be required to achieve the profit target set by the directors?

From the sales budget we can prepare the following budgets:

→ production budget

→ manufacturing budget, subdivided into materials budget, labour budget and manufacturing overheads budget

→ administration costs budget

→ selling and distribution costs budget

→ capital expenditure budget.

All these budgets start from the increased figure for sales and will call on last year's budget when setting the new one. These budgets may then be combined to give a budgeted profit and loss account, a cash budget and a budgeted balance sheet for the whole organisation.

Typically, the budgets building into the profit and loss account will be prepared for a year and analysed into quarterly or monthly periods. Some companies constantly update their budgets to plan 12 months ahead (a rolling budget). However, it is more common to plan once a year for the following financial year.

10 KEY PERFORMANCE INDICATORS

Companies and other organisations use key performance indicators (KPIs) to measure their progress towards achieving their goals and to make decisions for how to proceed. Typically, senior managers will set KPIs for the organisation as a whole, and agree them for each department within the organisation. Team leaders often agree KPIs for individual team members. For example, a hospital may have an objective to improve survival rates. For individual departments, this may become a target to reduce the time that patients have to wait to receive an appointment to see a consultant. For the appointments clerk, the target translates into a series of KPIs concerned with the number of appointments processed, the efficient use of the consultants' time and other factors that will have an impact on the low- and high-level KPIs.

KPIs are both an extension from and a distillation of the traditional management accounting system. They are an extension in the sense that they deal not only with financial matters but also with a range of non-financial measures as appropriate for the particular organisation. But KPIs will often be a distillation of the management information system, since they are frequently derived from the detailed information provided in voluminous management reports. For example, a sales manager may get the value of sales and profit made last month and have a KPI that the profitability – the ratio between the two – should be equal to or greater than 25%. One of the problems with this is that the KPIs are then subject to all the weaknesses inherent in the management information system – including the possibility that the data used in compiling the KPIs is inaccurate.

KPIs have received almost universal acclaim from management but are frequently derided by staff. There is no doubt that the theory behind KPIs is sound, but the practical application often leaves a lot to be desired. When setting and using KPIs in your organisation, try to keep the following in mind:

→ **Concentrate on key measures.** One of the authors joined a company where he was told that he had to achieve 56 different KPIs. Faced with too big a task, the employee will not even try. It is usually considered that the optimal number of KPIs for any individual is about five.

→ **Try to maintain balance.** Staff may give attention to the achievement of a single measure and lose sight of the bigger picture. One of the authors was sent an appointment date from the local hospital. Since the date was inconvenient, he tried to delay the appointment for a week but was told by the appointments clerk that this was unacceptable because it would then fall outside the target, which was to see all patients within four weeks. In one way the appointments clerk was right to try to enforce this time limit, bearing in mind the hospital's objective to improve survival rates, but since the condition was not life-threatening (we hope), the system of KPIs should be clever enough to allow the hospital to give consideration to the patient's convenience without failing in a key measure.

→ **Keep it simple – and beware manipulation.** Do the staff understand the measure and what it is trying to achieve? Do the staff know what they must do to reach the target set – and by legitimate means? Staff want to give good news to their boss – especially where the payment of a bonus is linked to the achievement of KPIs. A bar manager, for example, gained a reputation for turning round the profitability of bars he took over as a temporary manager. What he was actually doing was simply stopping any maintenance activity. If a chair broke, he put it in the cellar. He performed well in terms of his profitability KPI but was storing up problems for the people who came after. Many years ago, one of the authors worked for an organisation where managers were required to keep control over the amounts owed to the company by customers. The KPI used was debtors' days (see in Director's Toolkit on page 174) and the target was to reduce debtors' days to at most 30. The intention of the KPI was that managers would be motivated to chase customers for early payment. Instead, one of the managers achieved his debtors' target by an accounting fraud.

To help avoid some of the pitfalls discussed above, managers are urged to bear in mind the SMART acronym when setting KPIs:

→ specific

→ measurable

→ agreed

→ realistic

→ time-bound.

For example, a fundraiser for a charity may have a KPI that is 'To achieve a 10% rise in donation income over the next 12 months'.

STOP – THINK – ACT

Reflect on the top ten finance tools and techniques, and identify elements that you will include in your framework for finance.

What should we do?	What tools and techniques are appropriate?
Who do we need to involve?	Who needs to be involved and why?
What resources will we require?	What information, facilities, materials, equipment or budget will be required?
What is the timing?	How long will each activity typically take?

Visit **www.Fast-Track-Me.com** to use the Fast Track online planning tool.

Financial planning and value creation
Professor Kiran Virdee and Professor Carole Print

For many finance professionals the following steps in the annual planning cycle will be familiar:

→ An initial top-down corporate plan is developed by the corporate head office.

→ Senior management at the corporate office provides guidance and targets to each business unit.

→ Business units develop their own strategies and three- to five-year financial plans.

→ A review and challenge follows between the corporate head office and each business unit.

→ Once medium-term financial plans are approved, they are expanded in detail to construct next year's budget.

The planning cycle involves both operational and strategic planning, but often the reality is that the two elements are carried out in isolation of each other. Research with 11 large multinational organisations[1] identified the following:

→ Strategic planning and operational planning processes are generally standalone, as they are carried out by different departments, over different timescales and with different levels of detail.

→ Strategic planning is normally coordinated by a head of strategy based in the corporate office, while the finance department takes the lead in budgeting and performance monitoring processes.

→ Strategic planning normally takes place towards the middle of the financial year, while the budgeting process kicks in towards the last quarter of the year.

→ Most companies consider that strategy development and strategy formulation are happening on a continuous basis rather than being a one-off event; however, the preparation of three- to five-year strategy plans seems to be a one-off annual activity.

→ Strategy formulation is mainly the realm of senior management, while budgeting involves many people throughout the organisation.

→ The strategic planning time horizon is three to five years and the budget is 12 months, normally based on year 1 of the strategy plan.

→ In most companies there is an emphasis on the short term at the expense of the long term, a lack of ownership and trust, and poor communication.

[1] Print, C. and Virdee, K. (2006), *The Alignment Between Operational and Strategic Planning in Large Multinational Organisations*, Henley-on-Thames: Henley Working Paper Series, HWP0610.

The research also revealed that the majority of the practitioners were satisfied that there was alignment between their operational and strategic planning processes, confirming in general terms the planning cycle identified above, while demonstrating some areas where practice could be improved.

The following provides a number of logical and common-sense suggestions for organisations to improve the efficiency and effectiveness of their planning and budgeting processes. Most importantly, there needs to be leadership and commitment from the highest level, with senior management setting direction and guidelines, in a challenging and coaching role.

→ Keep the detail and effort in planning processes to a minimum. Keep it simple.

→ Encourage local autonomy and accountability instead of central control in planning processes.

→ Prepare rolling forecasts so that the planning horizon extends beyond the one-year budget period into future periods.

→ Aim to use the same measures for both short-term and long-term performance monitoring, recognising both financial and non-financial performance measures.

→ Direct management time and energy at managing future results, not explaining past performance. Clearly identify priorities and discuss resource deployment early.

→ Separate strategy reviews from discussions on budgets and financial targets. Debate assumptions and not forecasts.

→ Keep in mind that effective policies and procedures can help promote more effective actions, improved behaviours and better decision making. Use common databases, terms and rigorous frameworks.

→ Be aware that comprehensive and relevant communication is required, as those who formulate strategy may be different from those who implement it.

→ Base incentives and rewards on strategic goals, not only against annual budget targets. Strategic objectives should be included in performance appraisal systems, recognising the link between operational and financial metrics.

→ Drive performance 'holistically' – from five-year plans to annual budgets to monthly forecasts.

The potential prize for organisations that have effective alignment and linkage, and who adopt good planning principles in their processes, is the translation of strategy into real financial returns – which, if sustained over time, may enhance shareholder value.

4

TECHNOLOGIES

To remain as effective and efficient as possible, Fast Track managers differentiate themselves by the support mechanisms they put in place to help themselves and their team. These include the intelligent use of appropriate technologies – enabling, for example, the automation of non-core activities and thereby freeing up time to focus on managing, motivating and leading people.

Understanding the starting point

The one part of your organisation's computer systems you cannot avoid is the internal management accounting system. Spend time when you take over a new team to get to grips with the system and understand its strengths and weaknesses.

Sparring with the internal management system

Technology at its best can transform a team's ability to thrive and achieve success. On that optimistic note, let's look at the way technology works for your team now and how it might help more in the future.

The finance department got into computing at a very early stage. It was easy to justify the computerisation of the payroll system, for example, since the saving in manpower was enormous. Historically the finance department also owned the computers, and before the days of an IT department with an IT director it was the finance department that provided some sort of service to other parts of the business. So there is a long history of finance and technology. That history can also have a legacy – systems that are old and need to be replaced but still remain at the heart of the business. This is the main reason why the internal management accounting systems tend to be the opposite of an enabler and instead put obstacles in the way of managers and team leaders. One other reason is that accountants, who are very comfortable with a page full of figures and cannot understand why anyone else would want them presented any other way, often design the reports the system produces.

It is worthwhile, therefore, at a time when you are taking over a new team, or have responsibility for the financial side of the team's work, to take a long hard look at the internal management accounting systems to see whether they are playing their part in helping you to achieve the most that you can. After all, good or bad, you are lumbered with the current system until you take the initiative and push for change.

Test your system against the following criteria:

➔ **A good system is produced as the result of frequent and effective communication between the accountants and the managers of the business.** It is a flaw in many teams' planning process to bring the accountants into the plan too late. No finance department can react immediately to any single team's requirement for a different set of reporting information. Bring them in early and keep them involved. Get to know your financial controller – they can be terrific allies but, we have to remind you, an equally horrific enemy.

QUICK TIP *RELATIONSHIP WITH THE FINANCIAL CONTROLLER*

Take this very seriously. Frankly your job is to make the controller feel more a part of your team than they do of the finance department. Don't just ask them to the occasional team meeting but also invite them to social occasions – the summer barbeque, the team visit to the Newmarket races and the Christmas party. This is particularly effective if no one else does it.

→ **The system should not deal solely with the financial effects of what is happening.** Financial figures are what are known as lagging indicators. They tell what has gone wrong after the event. You need information that shows what is going wrong before it has a negative influence on the figures. Find out what information you require by asking the question, 'What factors are critical to my success?' Then make sure the system gives you data that tells you how that part of the operation is going. It is not necessarily financial figures. For example, if your team is mainly concerned with selling, then activity reporting – the number of calls each salesperson makes – would be useful as part of the internal control system.

→ **You must find the management accounts credible.** It is a fact of business life that if any measures are less than rigorous, someone will use them to the disadvantage of the organisation. It can be very difficult for a large organisation to provide credible information to all its managers. Your performance is going to be measured as it is reported in the management accounting system, so it's worth putting effort into getting the reported figures right and credible. Take a salesperson getting information on their sales. If there is something blaringly wrong that is going to mean that they will be paid less than they should be, they will appeal, and through their manager and the bonus scheme administrators they will make sure that they are paid the right amount. Meanwhile, the original information is still being used at a higher level to monitor performance. Another example comes if the people who designed the bonus scheme get anything slightly wrong; the salespeople will find it about an hour after the scheme is published and exploit the mistake for their own ends.

→ **The system should concentrate on as small a number of key measures as possible, so that managers can control all of them at the same time.** Most people keep the really important management control figures for their job in their heads. They roughly know before the reports come in how they are doing.

The art of management reporting is to capture these measures. There is also a limit to how many measures your boss can monitor, and you quickly get to know where an abundance of so-called controls have left loopholes through which the Fast Track manager can drive a coach and horse.

→ **A good system gives clear indications to managers and avoids delivering impenetrable lists of irrelevant numbers.** Managers should only receive the data that they need to run their part of the organisation. Sometimes managers spend a lot of time picking out the information they require from the load of information sent to them on a regular basis.

→ **A good system must assist in detecting the secondary effect of some trends in the numbers.** Sometimes numbers, which are looking good, are actually concealing a problem. For example, it is often true that an improvement in cash flow and revenues can mask a problem with the order book, unless all three are reported on and linked in some way.

→ **The system needs to show comparisons and trends as well as the absolute numbers.** This is more difficult in a seasonal business, when the real comparison that managers need is what is happening this year set against what happened last year, rather than the simpler number of last month against this.

So, how well does your management accounting system shape up? Include in your plans time to meet with the finance people to make the most urgent improvements that will have the biggest impact on your ability to succeed.

How do I free up time?

As a team leader your main job is to deliver against the objectives agreed with your boss – sell this amount of product, deliver this amount of service and come up with the innovative ideas that will take your company forward, or whatever. If you are being diverted from this main task by looking after the financial or administration side, then take a long hard look at how technology could free up some of that time.

Perhaps you should record your activities in some detail for a while to really understand how you are spending your time. This will help to point out places where you can use technology to increase your own productivity.

QUICK TIP *THINKING TIME*
Do not forget to build into your schedule time for you and the team to think.

Top technologies

How do I know what technology exists?

It is a fact of modern business life that your team needs to keep up with what relevant technology is available to assist you to achieve success. Try asking one person in the team – they usually select themselves – to give you regular reports on changes in technology that could help you. Give them an objective to write a one-page report on a monthly basis, which will be discussed at a team meeting.

What tools will support a sustainable approach to finance?

Remember that the development of technologies is moving so quickly that the list of what is available to you will never be static. Use the following list as a challenge to what is possible, but accept that is a snapshot of what is happening at a point in time. The key is to get into the habit of constantly scanning this field in search of ideas for improving the effectiveness and efficiency of your finance framework.

1 Finance-oriented websites

| **What are they?** | The internet has opened up a myriad of opportunities to gain knowledge and improve your and your team's skills in the area of finance. From financial information to industry averages, it's all on the internet. There are two ways of getting information from the web – often referred to as 'push' and 'pull'. Traditionally we go to a website and pull relevant information off as required. However, increasingly we can request to have information 'pushed' at us, using streaming technologies. For example, many people now have the latest stock prices or updates on the weather sent to their desktops on a regular basis. Others will get competitive product information when it is announced. |

Pros	If you want to keep up to date with matters financial, then the site at **www.ft.com** can be invaluable. There is a lot of information available without registering, and a whole lot more if you register and log in. When logged in you can access, for example, financial information about companies that is more up to date than their annual report. Also available on the web are industry average figures that allow you to compare a company whose figures you are studying with the average performance in its industry – try **www.accountingweb.co.uk/icc**. You can also use the internet for distance learning; there are many finance courses available, from the basics to degree level.
Cons	Most of the information contains a degree of bias. After all, someone has produced it for their own purposes. The internet is also quite unstructured in that a search on a topic will yield lots of results but the information on each site will be laid out in a different style. Some people call it a repository of several trillion words; the trouble is locating the 25 words you really need.
Success factors	Use the web as a rich source of information and get into the habit of reviewing competitor and customer sites regularly. Beware of information overload, and if new information is of critical importance then validate your conclusions using other sources. A neat rule of thumb is the one that journalists use – only publish a 'fact' if you have got at least two reliable sources.

2 Online access to company reports

What is it?	Companies have been publishing accounts on their websites for some time. In the past this was seen as the provision of information to potential customers and investors, but it was not the primary means of communicating with existing shareholders. In December 2000 the Companies Act was amended to allow companies to communicate electronically with their members. Further revisions in the Companies Act 2006 have made it compulsory for quoted companies to make the annual report and accounts available on a website.
Pros	From the point of view of a major company, this offers an opportunity of cost savings on printing and postage. It will still need to inform the members that the accounts are available on the website, but this can be done by a postcard or, with the agreement of each member, an email. The most obvious implication of this is that the glossy brochure containing the annual report and accounts will no longer be sent as a matter of course to all members.
	From the point of view of someone wanting access to the report, the benefit is that they do not have to wait until a report reaches them by post and they can access a lot of reports in a short period of time.

Cons	The reason that the annual report has become more and more concerned with glamour and spin is that it is also used as a promotional tool – and that benefit is now going to be lost. However, it could be argued that the attempt to make the annual report more interesting to shareholders by the inclusion of additional information has resulted in the accounting requirements being relegated to the back of the booklet. Perhaps the annual accounts have become submerged within the promotional document. On the other hand, getting hold of the actual report does tell you a lot about the company's approach to marketing its brand: some companies will go for a utility, non-glossy branding, others for a work of art. Websites give you the opportunity to dodge around the information as the fancy takes you. The problem with this is that at one moment the reader of the accounts will be looking at audited material – true and fair, under the watchful eye of the auditor – and the next they will be transported to advertising literature containing hype. Will they realise that this information does not have the seal of the auditor's approval? The websites must also be secure, so that no one can amend the accounts accidentally or as part of a fraud. How often do the directors (or auditors) check that the information is still valid?
Success factors	The reader of the online annual report will not start at the beginning with the glossy photographs of the board and the chairman's view of the year. Rather, they will select from a menu to read the sections they are really interested in.

 CASE STORY *PLANT AND MACHINERY, CHRISTINE'S STORY*

Narrator Christine is a salesperson. Her main customer is a large food processing company.

Context Christine works for a small company that is in a state of flux about its future strategy. She could not resource more than one sales campaign for her key customer.

Issue Christine felt her prospects were better in the subsidiary that sold cakes and biscuits because the people there were more enthusiastic. The frozen foods subsidiary also had a need for her product, but they were less advanced in their thinking and planning.

Solution To help decide where to put the effort in, she read the company's group annual report online and found that the board's strategy was moving away from bakery and into frozen products. She put her resources into the frozen foods company and eventually took an order after a difficult campaign. Later, the board sold off half of the bakery division and shut the other half.

Learning Think about things from the point of view of your customers, not only now but in the future. The top-level strategy of an organisation can tell you a lot about how lower divisions will act.

3 Corporate e-trading

What is it?	Like so many other products and commodities, companies can now trade shares on the internet. Despite some concerns about security, which the industry has more or less overcome, there has been a huge upsurge in the proportion of share transactions taking place on the internet. Once you have set up an account it is very convenient.
Pros	The stockbroking business has become very competitive, and online trading offers reductions in costs to the stockbroker that can be and are passed on to the investor in the form of lower transaction charges. Transaction charges are an important element in any share deal, and the investor is well advised to look for the best deal they can get in order to maximise the return on their investment. The internet offers not only the means of buying and selling shares, but also easy access to complex trades such as hedging and spread betting on more or less a seven-days-a-week, 24-hours-a-day basis. More and more people therefore make a principal hobby or even a profession out of day trading – speculating on the online market in an attempt to make capital profits in a very short time and very frequently. The evidence for their success, it is sobering to realise, is thin. There is better evidence that says that the grand majority of day traders lose money, often very quickly.
Cons	Perhaps its greatest strength is also its weakness. Buying shares by going to a bank or a stockbroker takes time during the working day, and an internet account solves that. But it also means that it is all too easy to press a button and buy or sell: impulse-buying of shares does not look like a likely source of wealth. As they say, 'To make a small fortune on the stock exchange, start with a large one.'
Success factors	Assuming you have absolute confidence in a site's security, look for ones that are easy to use and give you easy access to how your portfolio is performing.

QUICK TIP *BE SECURITY CONSCIOUS*
Keep passwords and PIN numbers secret from everyone. Don't use the same password for everything. Remember, no one in Nigeria is actually holding millions of dollars that can be yours for the asking. And banks never, ever ask for security information by email.

4 Sharing insights and information

What is it?
Consider the example of a manager of a training academy in a major telecommunications company, who has expressed the view that the biggest problem, or opportunity, facing them is how to pass learning from the engineers and others working on one project to the people tackling a similar project later on. This includes the financial implications of actions taken and not taken. The technology dimension here is obvious, in that information recorded on the company intranet is available instantly to other people around the world.

Pros
If everyone uses the same tool for analysing an annual report, for example, on the intranet there can be a consistent view of the financial data concerning your competitors, your customers and your suppliers. All it requires is for finance people to agree on a simple tool, such as the one starting on page 167, and then for people to make use of it.

Cons
Involving people is a problem. How do you motivate people to enter the data in the first place and then keep it up to date?

Success factors
Ease of use and ease of access are essential if you are to promote the sharing of ideas and insights. Someone needs to be responsible for making sure that people are keeping intranet information up to date.

5 Forums

What are they?
Taking the use of the intranet a stage further, the forum becomes an important part of a technology-based knowledge centre. A forum is a special website that allows people to log in and discuss ideas relating to a specific topic in the form of a discussion thread, where the most recent comments are displayed first. Forums may be created on the internet or on the company intranet, and provide a place where groups of people internal or external to the organisation can share ideas.

Pros	Here like-minded individuals can analyse the reports of their own company or those of other organisations. A forum is also useful in an environment where widespread teams are working on the same customers. For example, a person about to make contact with the Australian subsidiary of an American company can check on the intranet for an analysis of the report of the target company, prior to joining the forum set up to disseminate information about the global company. Forums work particularly well where they are focused on a specific topic, like the financial implications of teams' activities. These are sometimes referred to as special interest groups or SIGs.
Cons	Unless there is a clear reason for going to the forum, many people just don't bother, so a team leader has to encourage their team to use it and build it into their normal processes. Forums probably work best for IT teams, where there is already a culture of sharing insights and expertise, but may not work so well with other functions.
Success factors	Consider carefully whether you would use a forum, and if so how? What would make it exciting and worthwhile enough to make it work within the company, when most people will have other commitments to focus on? Perhaps find a small team that would be interested in piloting a forum on a specific topic and see how they get on.

6 Business case template

What is it?	An up-to-date business case template can be made available on the intranet, explaining what type of project the company is looking for. It explains the criteria that are used to judge a business case – for example, one that requires capital expenditure. Against the criteria are weightings that the company will use to test a project. A company seeking growth, for example, might give a high weighting to projects aimed at increasing sales, while one moving towards cash flow problems will prefer projects that impact cash flow favourably and quickly.
Pros	Perhaps there is no other area in a company where the wheel is reinvented as many times as in putting together a business case. Similarly, in no other area is as much time wasted as in putting together reports that recommend projects that are just never going ahead. The business case template can save a lot of time for a lot of people.
Cons	As with any objective test, people will find emotional reasons and reasons of urgency to dispute the weightings. The potential project sponsor will use phrases like 'This is not optional' and 'To be competitive, we have just got to do it'.

Success factors	You need a balance between the objective criteria that check that a project is within the company strategy, and more subjective opinions concerning the way the market or the products are going. The business template criteria are an aid to decision making but are not the decision maker.

7 Return on investment tool

What is it?	It is quite possible to make a return on investment tool available electronically. It is a simple model recording the steps in choosing a timescale, estimating costs and benefits and then producing the profit and loss account, cash flow and discounted cash flow. You can also use such a tool for risk analysis and decision making.
Pros	Such a consistent approach to making a business case is extremely helpful to the managers who have to decide between one project and another. In addition, people can look at previous business cases and learn from them.
Cons	Take care it is not a sledgehammer to crack a nut. The first time people use this tool may be quite daunting and, of course, some people will become good at using it while others will shy away. The problem comes when one of the reasons senior managers choose between projects is the skill of the person filling in the model.
Success factors	Offer lots of support and training in using the tool. Get the finance people involved early on in making the business case, rather than having them come in late and rubbish the work already done.

8 Spreadsheet applications

What are they?	Spreadsheet systems really brought the power of the computer into the hands of the managers and team leaders who actually produce products, services and sales for a company. These applications not only make it simple to manipulate data and formulae but they also can go much further than that – for example, allowing users to create databases, link spreadsheets together and perform mathematical and financial functions. It is quite likely that even an experienced user only uses a small fraction of the features available in the system, but that's the point – you use the bits that give you what you want.
Pros	Use these applications for creating and monitoring budgets, sales forecasting, calculating return on investment, analysing annual reports – and more. In fact, if as a team leader you do not have reasonable skills in creating spreadsheets, you are fighting the financial part of your battle with one arm tied behind your back. Spreadsheets are also terrific learning tools. For example, if you are not sure about how to raise a profit and loss account, try to do it on a spreadsheet and then go over it with a financial controller; you will soon understand the profit and loss perfectly well.

Cons	Their strength of being fun and easy to use can lead to the weakness of soaking up a lot of line managers' time, trying to create the perfect spreadsheet. Make sure that you use the system as an enabler and don't allow it to become a hindrance.
Success factors	The key success factor is that you do it yourself. The spreadsheet was created to get managers out of the clutches of the finance department, who previously were the only people who could devise the programmes necessary to do what we now do with spreadsheets. Don't replace a dependency on the finance department with a dependency on the IT department: take time out to learn what you need to know about spreadsheets and their application.

QUICK TIP *DON'T DEVALUE THE CURRENCY*

If a project fails against a set of rules of financial evaluation, consider changing the project rather than changing the rules.

9 Email

What is it?	Electronic mail allows members of a team to communicate via their computers. This has become the standard form of communication across and within businesses, and is a key tool for effective communications. Particularly useful in relation to finance is the ability of managers to send a one-line email pointing out to a team member that they are moving towards a problem with their budget. This is much less serious than making a phone call. Email says to the team member, 'I know that you can sort this out,' while a phone call says, 'OK, I'm stepping in and taking control.'
Pros	Most organisations already have email systems, with many being free of charge. Furthermore, even though they are complex, most people are so familiar with them that they are comfortable using them. (When email was first released the CEO of one of the top FTSE 100 companies said that it would never take off.)
Cons	Unfortunately, most email systems are open to a certain amount of abuse. First, there may be a tendency to copy people in unnecessarily to keep them informed – so creating internal junk mail. This wastes a significant amount of management time and attention. Alternatively, it is all too easy to communicate one on one without including other key stakeholders in the discussion. Using email can also slow down decisions. For example, we know one manager who got very fed up

with a lengthy email argument between two people who worked within sight of each other. He went to their desks, propelled them into a conference room equipped with coffee and Danish pastries, and told them not to come out until they had made a decision they were both comfortable with. Then he locked the door. A bit harsh maybe, but you can see his point.

Success factors Use email selectively to direct members of the team and to communicate with key stakeholders.

STOP – THINK – ACT

Now stop. Before going out and investing in the latest and greatest technical devices, remember that technology is just an enabler. Success will ultimately depend on your ability to lead the team, your behaviour and how you interact with others. Be wary of being drawn into new technologies too quickly – let someone else make the mistakes, but then learn quickly. Finally, if you do decide to introduce new systems to your team, think carefully about the possible risks – what could go wrong? Ask yourself and the team these questions:

What should we do?	What technologies are available that will help to improve effectiveness and efficiency?
Who do we need to involve?	Who would benefit and why?
What resources will we require?	What level of investment would be required?
What is the timing?	When would be a good time to introduce the new technology – is there a 'window of opportunity'?

Visit www.Fast-Track-Me.com to use the Fast Track online planning tool.

What is the financial value of people?

Professor Carole Print

" One of the key functions of finance is as the guardian of financial reporting – here we consider the reporting of what is often referred to as an organisation's 'most valuable asset'.

The value of a company is often considered to be the value of its assets. There has been considerable debate about the role of people as a vital asset in organisations, whether in the private or public sector, and a recognition that their skills and their knowledge are crucial contributors to the competitive advantage and profitability of a business. However, from a financial reporting perspective, there has been no generally accepted procedure for measuring the quality and effectiveness of human capital, and there has similarly been little obligation placed on companies by key regulators of the UK financial reporting system to report on human capital.

This is out of line with the increasing pressure on financial managers to demonstrate to boards and investors how human capital is being managed. Financial directors are also voicing their frustration at their inability to measure the return on investment in employees and want a greater role in managing human capital, which is seen as a major business driver. A more serious and full disclosure of this critical asset is required.

The decision late in 2005 by the UK's Chancellor of the Exchequer to scrap the Operating and Financial Review (OFR) took away the obligation for an element of 'reporting on people', although many companies decided to continue with their reporting of the requirements of the OFR. Even without the OFR, UK registered companies are still obliged to meet many of its requirements in the Business Review through the provisions of the 2003 EU Accounts Modernisation Directive. However, at issue is the non-mandatory stance taken of the requirements, which has led to a lack of consistent and full disclosure of what is so often reported in a company's annual report as its 'most valuable asset' – people.

Evidence from research into the reporting of human capital in annual accounts[1] shows the following:

[1] Print, C. (2007), *Are People Really Important? A Study of the External Reporting of Human Capital in UK Annual Accounts*, Henley-on-Thames: Henley Working Paper Series, HWP0712.

→ The reporting is predominantly narrative in style, with little quantification of statements or demonstration of the quality of the company commitment to the item reported, or the degree/quality of benefit achieved.

→ Although there are developments by some companies to increase the amount of information, it is generally difficult to make an assessment of whether and how a company is using and creating value from its human capital base.

→ There is little evidence that companies are taking human capital reporting seriously. Reporting is patchy and found in a number of locations, with usually no central repository for the information on employees. If companies are going to 'walk the talk', the reporting needs to be comprehensive and cohesive.

→ Unsurprisingly, the most reported areas are those that are mandatory, which calls into question the non-mandatory nature of requirements – are many companies only going to report what is mandatory and not what is 'recommended' and voluntary?

To sum up, there is generally limited reporting of this critical asset to users of accounts and those interested in understanding how companies manage and measure their performance. Issues such as the quality of the workforce and how they create value are not at all well documented. Yet if directors are of the view that people are important and a critical asset, it must be the case that reporting on them in their annual review is relevant and unavoidable. It becomes a business imperative for companies to accept both the opportunity and the challenge this presents, to develop a valuable and informative non-financial disclosure framework of human capital.

5

IMPLEMENTING CHANGE

There is no one right way to create a sustainable approach to the financial element of your job. You will need to decide for yourself what is and is not appropriate for your team and business. When you have decided on the changes you need to make, you still need to think ahead and plan the changes carefully.

Planning the financial way ahead

In the end, you and your team are judged by financial results. This means that you need to get everyone's attitude to finance right and make sure that they can use any new financial tools and methods that you are bringing into play. This requires change, and generally speaking people do not like change. Here is some advice on getting acceptance to the changes you need to drive through to make sure the team is operating on all financial cylinders.

Making a plan

How do we get their attitude right?

A sales director hired Ken as a consultant to talk to his first- and second-line managers about finance – a classic finance for non-financial managers' task. Ken asked him what was driving him to do this and how he wanted the managers to change. His reply was, 'Make them spend the company's money as though it were their own.' As an encapsulation of getting the team's attitude to money right, that seems as good as any.

Emphasise to the team that just because they are working for an organisation does not mean that its money can be spent as though it were free, like a victimless crime. Involve them in the profit-making process by explaining how your profit centre is measured and judged. A good way of doing this is to make a cost cut that hurts or even irritates them. Some managers believe in the old 'take away the free coffee and biscuits' ploy. The team will moan, giving you the opportunity to fix their attitude.

Here's how it works. Explain your budget and show how most team leaders have a budget with very little discretionary spend. Indeed you can probably prove that 95% of your budget is not discretionary. That 95% covers staff costs, accommodation costs and the team's contribution to overheads. So in a £1 million budget only £50,000 can be spent how the leader wants – on things like travel, expenses, stationery, parties and, of course, free biscuits. Assuming that the team does not want to make a cut in staff, you can then ask them to look for cost savings and offer to reinstate free coffee and biscuits if they produce a saving to cover it. They may very well try to do this – if they do, you have made a big step forward in getting their attitude right.

CASE STORY PACKAGE HOLIDAY COMPANY, DERRICK'S STORY

Narrator Derrick is the financial director of a package holiday company.

Context The package holiday industry runs on very low gross and net profit margins. It can only thrive if everyone is aware of this and keeps very tight control of costs.

Issue Senior managers were having difficulty getting the teams to realise that small changes in performance have a dramatic effect on the bottom line. The teams still believed that if sales went down by a very small percentage it could not do much harm.

Solution Derrick got all the people involved together and in a lecture showed them the reality of small changes. He explained how if costs go up by just 2% while sales volume goes down by just 2%, and you give a discount of just 2%, then the overall impact is that profits go down by a whopping 46%. 'If, however,' he went on, 'these three crucial figures improve by 2%, then profits go up by the same whopping 46%.'

Learning Businesses thrive on the margin. Make your team aware that there is no such thing as a negligible adverse financial change and keep a tight control on the financial side of what you are doing. While the 46% figure is particular to the facts of this case, the impact of small changes is always significant in any business.

Putting a plan together

Senior managers are responsible for making sure that the company's financial systems and processes are integrated. They must ensure, for example, that the activities of one division do not compete with or harm another division. But your role at this stage is to make sure that the financial activities in your team are fit for purpose. You may need to make changes to all or some of the three main financial areas. This involves:

→ sorting out the internal management accounting system;

→ using annual reports for research;

→ introducing return on investment calculations to check on the feasibility of projects and other activities.

We look at these in some detail below.

However, things change. Plan how to implement your financial framework but keep an eye on what other teams and divisions are doing. Keeping in touch with the rest of the business is important for achieving your results, as well as developing your career.

Implementing your financial framework

Sorting out the internal management accounting system

The best people to advise you on the effectiveness of the internal accounting system are the people in the team who have been using it for a while and, of course, your predecessor. If possible, speak to your predecessor before calling a meeting of the whole team. Ask the team,

'Do we have access to the right financial information at the right time and is it accurate?' Given that aim of the system, ask the team to identify the strengths and weaknesses of the current way of doing things.

Look for make do and mend – extrapolations that team members do on a regular basis to work out what the actual position is when they get their internal financial reports. Allocation of costs is often a good example of this. Team members get the report showing what they spent against budget in the last month and go through it picking out the errors, so that they can work out what their real spend was. They know that eventually costs allocated in error will be corrected, but they need to do that work to make sure they are not in any danger of blowing their budget. It would, of course, be far more efficient if the system was amended to get it right in the first place. Look also for information that the team is simply 'doing without', knowing that if they had it then their decision making and activities would be more productive.

Make a list of the places that need to be improved and then do an ABC analysis on it, where those marked A are the urgent ones that have the worst effect on the team and those marked C are the least urgent. Don't expect to get all the changes done at once, so perhaps limit yourself to achieving the changes on the A list.

You will probably encounter resistance from the people who have been around for a while, who will explain to you that the current system is a fact of life and that you will not be able to change it. Explain back that such an attitude is self-fulfilling and that the whole team is going to strive to get change. Sometimes it is a good idea to put a member of the team in charge of chasing these changes, but remember to keep yourself well in the loop.

QUICK TIP LOOK FOR OTHER MEASURES

As you encourage your team to look for improvement in the internal systems, get them to think of other indicators apart from finance that would be useful. If, for example, they see a need to improve customer service, suggest that the monthly report should include the number of complaints, service times, etc.

Using annual reports for research

If your team really has no knowledge of how to analyse an annual report, you will almost certainly have to splash out on some training for them. They can easily learn to do it in a couple of days with a good trainer, but your job is to make sure they keep the knowledge up by using it once they come back from the classroom.

Make sure they really appreciate the benefits of doing such an analysis on all their contacts:

→ **Customers.** Analysing a customer's annual report is a boon both to selling and to after-sales service. This is true even when the customer concerned is an internal one, such as the IT department. The team will ask better questions after they have done the analysis and will have a better idea of which of your products and services are likely to be vital for the customer in the future. The analysis will also ensure that the team is directing its effort in the best possible area of the customer's business.

→ **Suppliers.** Analysing the reports of suppliers is not a credit check – there is someone in the finance department who does that – but is a check that both companies are going in a compatible direction and that you make best use of any influence you have over the supplier's strategy.

→ **Competitors.** There is much to learn by studying the outward face of a competitor.

The above list covers just some of the benefits of this research. You can increase the motivation process by asking the team to add their own benefits. Make sure they look at the benefits from all angles, particularly the 'What's in it for me?' angle.

Work out the benefits of using these analytical skills to each individual team member, the team itself and the organisation:

→ Individuals who improve their ability to work with, understand and manipulate financial data not only improve performance in the short term but also make a career step forward by learning a vital skill. If they don't do it now, when are they going to get a good knowledge of the financial side of business? They certainly won't get on the board without it, so they may as well do it now. It's simply a matter of being more professional.

→ **The team will produce better results**. Sometimes these improvements will be specific and sometimes more general. Specifically, studying a supplier strategy may show that a product you are buying from them is going to be phased out. This allows you to negotiate new discounts for the remaining stocks, as well as making the case for not spending any more on the new replacement product. Generally, the team will learn business skills that will certainly make them look at what they are doing in a different light and come up with suggestions for improvement.

→ **The organisation benefits from the better results of the team, which is demonstrating extra professionalism to suppliers and customers**. If senior managers appreciate what the team is doing, they may well use their methods as a template for building the skills in other parts of the business.

Using investment appraisal techniques

This is another area offering huge potential to improve the results of your team. What you are suggesting is that the experts in the team – be they marketers, engineers, salespeople or whatever – are going to add another string to their bow by understanding in advance what the business will gain from any project that they would like to do or even that they are in the middle of doing. While the case for the project may initially be overwhelming, a competitor may bring out something that is two keystrokes better than your product. It is much better for the business if there is a sound financial case with a complete risk analysis accompanying it.

If the team has not done this before you will have to arrange a training session. During this it can be useful to take an existing project where some of the uncertainties are removed and do a justification for the spend. From here you can move on to testing potential projects or opportunities for investing money in new activities. Some teams do not attempt to do the financial side, but this puts all of your projects in jeopardy – when times get tough, the sound business case is king. Other teams let the financial people do the case. This is like allowing a referee to rewrite the rulebook to favour whichever side they want to win. You have to know what the finance people are doing and how they are doing it if you are to have some control over your destiny.

Look again for what is in it for the team members, the team and the organisation:

→ **The individual will be able to put good financial logic behind whatever projects and activities they feel passionate about**. They improve their business skills and make themselves more valuable as a result. If they understand what the financial people are doing when they apply investment appraisal techniques, they are much less likely to be blinded by any financial jargon.

→ **The team will secure its future**. If you have a financial payback for what you are doing agreed with senior management, then you can sleep quietly in the knowledge that your team will be left to complete the tasks in hand. You will also be in the pole position for resources if any become spare, which could speed up the financial benefits that completion of your project offers.

→ **The organisation is greater than the sum of its parts**. This is particularly the case when its professionals are multiskilled – when they have their specialist expertise and also understand the business issues.

QUICK TIP ESTIMATE BENEFITS
When you are valuing a benefit that is hard for a manager to estimate, try asking them whether it would be a low number; if they reply that it must be more than that, try them with a high number: now you've begun to narrow them down.

Ensuring success – keeping the plan on track

What approach should we use?

Ideally you want a plan with a series of actions involving every member of the team. It should have at least three milestones for each of the three areas of change that you are putting in place. For example, one milestone could be the date by which you will be in a position to present your request for changes to the internal management reporting system.

Integrate the actions with the training. For example, when you are doing the training on reading annual reports make sure that you have a model that the teams will use for both the strategy identification and the financial analyses. Ensure that the models prepared during the training session are available on the intranet so that people can see each other's progress as they input data on the chosen companies and examine the results.

You can do exactly the same when completing the business case, the risk analysis model and the financial cash flow forms.

What routines should we set up?

Agree with the team the circumstances in which they will use the financial tools in Chapter 3. The key is to have a routine where they do a little often. Regular use of the tools not only sustains learning but also massively improves their ability to use them quickly and effectively. They will know what useful information they are going to get out of each use of the tools, and slowly but surely they will, become better professionals as a result.

Keep routines flexible so that people feel they are learning and using financial techniques because of the benefits they bring to them and the team rather than ticking a box in their personal development plan. But put processes in place. It is very difficult to get people to agree to change unless they are working to a process that everyone has bought into. If the team takes a common approach to finance, teamwork improves and the decisions arrived at are the result of the activities and thinking of the whole team.

>
> QUICK TIP **POST HOC JUSTIFICATION**
> If you come up with a comparison of the costs and benefits for an existing project where the benefits heavily outnumber the costs, look for more opportunities of the same type.

Critical success factors

So how can we increase our chances of success?

Managing change can be a depressing business, but there is hope. Research in production and other environments supports a rule of thumb that we have found to be true practically: if you have to manage a change process, you need 'agents of change' to support you. Agents of change are people who fundamentally agree with the need for change and have the will to go through the process themselves.

We have found in practice that if 20% of the people involved in the change will act as your agents of change, then your chances of success are good. Less than 10% and you may have to drop your aspirations a bit until you have got more support.

To a large degree change management, for that is what this really is, is about overcoming resistance and people's fears and objections to your plan. You have to be well prepared when implementing changes in a business, as not everyone will think like you. You have to deal with people's resistance to change, not try to prevent it.

To that end many successful managers have adopted the DREC curve as a means of understanding people's attitudes to your changes. DREC stands for the four 'emotions' you may come across while introducing change – for example, a new financial management framework:

→ **Denial.** The way we handle finance now will meet our needs for another few years.

→ **Resistance.** It is too expensive to change the framework.

→ **Exploration.** But we could alter that bit to begin with.

→ **Commitment.** This is a much better way of working.

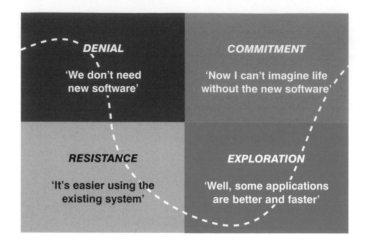

In the figure above the statements illustrate reactions to an event; what is important is the curve through the four quadrants. How you manage these reactions is crucial to the smooth implementation of change. So, in the example of the introduction of new financial routines, you could try the following strategies:

→ **Denial.** Initially the team might say, 'We don't need a financial management framework' or 'This framework will be a waste of time and effort'. They see their jobs as specialists in their own discipline and will baulk at this extra dimension. This is particularly true of finance because some people claim to have numeric or financial blindness. At this stage many comments are emotional and not rational and are borne out of fear of change. It is often best to allow colleagues to get their fears off their chest and allow them a 'rant' at this stage. Your role as leader of the team is to get through this stage as quickly and as painlessly as possible, *not* to hit their denial head on, which may only prolong matters and create opponents.

→ **Resistance.** At this stage there may be a tacit acceptance of the need for change, but its relevance may be limited to the individual in question. 'The framework may be useful to you, but not for my department' or 'Well, you'll have to do it in your time and with your resources, as it's not needed by my team' are the statements you may hear at this stage. Your role as the leader of the initiative is to get resisters to understand the benefits of your approach and to get them at least to explore certain scenarios and opportunities.

→ **Exploration.** Your role at this stage is to expand the areas in which the resister might find your financial management framework useful, albeit on a limited scale. It may be about selling to the individual the benefits of the framework and showing how it might solve problems for them. It may be about getting them to use the framework on a limited basis or piloting it for a limited time only – a taster with no commitment at this stage.

→ **Commitment.** Ultimately this is where we are trying to get people to – an acceptance that your framework is fundamental to the running of the business, which in fact they could not do without. However, don't look for praise or reward, as this may be another uphill struggle. Your reward should be the implementation of your initiative.

In summary, people using the DREC curve talk about the leaders' role being that of getting people to the fourth quadrant as quickly and as painlessly as possible, but having to go through the three previous quadrants first. There is no jumping quadrants – no easy jump from denial to commitment. Once you understand how resistance to change manifests itself, you can focus on the process by which you implement your plan.

QUICK TIP *YOU CAN'T WIN 'EM ALL*
If you are trying to change how a team operates, allow for the fact that you are going to fail with some people. Accept that they are not going to change but stop them hindering others. Then solve the problem of what to do with them.

Finally, communicate successes or 'quick wins' to all interested stakeholders, so that people can see that the overall approach is working and worthwhile.

STOP – THINK – ACT

Use the audit template in the Director's Toolkit on page 163 and identify the gaps in your approach to finance. Then identify what you will need to do to make your approach succeed.

What should we do?	What stages and tasks are appropriate?
Who do we need to involve?	Who needs to be involved and why?
What resources will we require?	What information, facilities, materials, equipment or budget will be required?
What is the timing?	How long will each activity typically take?

Visit www.Fast-Track-Me.com to use the Fast Track online planning tool.

EXPERT VOICE

Consortium stretches the limits of hostile takeover
Dr Giampiero Favato

In October 2007 the Royal Bank of Scotland Group (RBS) consortium, which also included Banco Santander SA of Spain and the Belgian-Dutch bank Fortis NV, claimed victory when it acquired control of ABN Amro after a seven-month battle against Barclays.[1]

The RBS takeover of ABN Amro is now seen as contributing to its downfall and a disaster for a once strong bank. However, the principles behind the approach it adopted may be seen as setting a trend for future takeovers. The charge against RBS is more about its due diligence and valuation rather than the approach itself.

Why does the approach still have relevance? Firstly recession creates opportunities for the bold. Mergers and acquisitions (M&A) activities will continue also because it ignites the creativity of the investment bankers advising corporate clients. It has long been a dream of M&A strategists to pick apart conglomerates composed of diversified divisions, and the consortium bid allows acquirers to pay a higher price and allocate pieces of the target to buyers who most value those assets. As a result, an entire tier of corporate holdings previously thought out of reach could become potential bid targets.

Conglomerates are companies that either partially or fully own a number of other companies, which may be in the same or in different industries. Titan holdings, such as General Electric or Unilever, were built up over many years, with interests ranging from avionics to premium ice cream. The case for conglomerates can be summed up in one word: diversification. According to financial theory, because the business cycle affects industries in different ways, diversification results in a reduction of investment risk. A downturn suffered by one subsidiary, for instance, can be counterbalanced by stability, or even expansion, in another venture.

Conglomerates do not always offer investors an advantage in terms of diversification. If investors want to diversify risk, they can do so themselves by investing in a few 'pure players' rather than investing in a single conglomerate. Investors can do this far more cheaply and efficiently than even the most acquisitive conglomerate can. The case against conglomerates is a strong one. Consequently, the market usually applies a discount to the sum-of-parts value – that is, it frequently values conglomerates at a discount to more focused companies.[1]

The calculation of the discount can be exemplified by using a fictional conglomerate called InGlobe plc, which consists of two unrelated businesses: a media division and a fine chemicals division. InGlobe plc has a market capitalisation of £4 billion and total debt of £1.5 billion. Its media division has balance sheet assets of £2 billion, while its fine chemicals division has £1.5 billion worth of assets. Focused companies in the media industry have median market-to-book values of 2.5, while pure-play fine chemical firms have market-to-book values of 2. InGlobe plc's divisions are fairly typical companies in their industries. From this information, we can calculate the conglomerate discount:

Total market value InGlobe plc:
= Equity + Debt
= £4 billion + £1.5 billion
= £5.5 billion

Estimated value sum of the parts:
= Value of fine chemicals division + Value of media division
= (£1.5 billion × 2) + (£2 billion × 2.5)
= £3 billion + £5 billion
= £8 billion

The conglomerate discount amounts to (£8 billion – £5.5 billion)/£8 billion
= 31.25%

[1] Mansi, S.A. and Reeb, D.M. (2002), 'Corporate diversification: what gets discounted?' *Journal of Finance*, 5(5), 2167–83.

It becomes clear that this multi-business company could be worth significantly more if it were broken up into individual businesses. Consequently, investors may push for divesting or spinning off its media and fine chemicals divisions to create more value.

Senior executives are also being pressured to deliver shareholder returns, as the investment base of companies shifts from passive institutional investors with longer-term horizons to hedge funds focused on the short term. Even though shareholder activism is generally considered to be positive because it makes companies more efficient and increases shareholder returns, some analysts believe that the focus on short-term returns can mean important long-term goals get neglected.

With the passage of time, the three buyers of ABN Amro have been found guilty of grossly overpaying for the deal which even at the time raised eyebrows. Given the general collapse in the banking sector, however, one might suggest that they were also caught out by changes in the business environment which were unforeseen by many other leading industry figures.

The approach, however, will no doubt prove attractive to other conglomerates in the future.

CAREER
FAST TRACK

Whatever you have decided to do in terms of developing your career as a manager, to be successful you need to take control, plan ahead and focus on the things that will really make a difference.

The first ten weeks of a new role will be critical. Get them right and you will be off to a flying start and will probably succeed. Get them wrong and you will come under pressure and even risk being moved on rather quickly. Plan this initial period to make sure you are not over-whelmed by the inevitable mass of detail that will assail you on arrival. Make sure that other people's priorities do not put you off the course that you have set yourself.

Once you have successfully eased yourself into your new role and gained the trust of your boss and the team, you can start to make things happen. First, focus on your leadership style and how it needs to change to suit the new role; then focus on the team. Are they the right people and, if so, what will make them work more effectively as a finance-oriented team?

Finally, at the appropriate time, you need to think about your next career move, and whether you are interested in getting to the top by becoming a company director. This is not for everyone, as the commitment, time and associated stress can be offputting, but the sense of responsibility and leadership can be enormously rewarding.

So far you've concentrated on performance – now it's time to look at your Fast Track career.

6

THE FIRST TEN WEEKS

The first ten weeks of starting a new role as the leader of a team are probably the most critical – get them wrong and you risk failure, get them right and you will enjoy and thrive in your new role. What do you need to do, where should you focus, what must you avoid at all costs and where does finance fit into all of this?

To take control, the Fast Track manager will seek to understand key facts, build relationships and develop simple mechanisms for monitoring and control – establishing simple but effective team processes. Again, this task will be simplified using modern technologies and so will become effortless and part of day-to-day behaviour.

Changing roles

Of course, it is likely in your first ten weeks in a new role that you will give priority to the functional purpose of the team. But it is also vital not to delay coming to grips with the financial element of the job. Build knowledge and skills for both areas at the same time.

Why is this a critical time?

In financial terms these first weeks are vital, since if you fail to signal that you want to make changes in how the team handles the financial side, people will make assumptions that you are content with everything as it is now. So during this period you need to get sufficiently up to speed to be able to put a plan together for a new way of handling finance, or at least to be in a position to signal that you are not satisfied with the status quo.

You need to communicate your intentions to both the financial controllers around you and the team itself. If, for example, you discover that very little work is done on the financial planning of projects and activities then you must indicate that change is coming and that you are going to get the team to reskill in a number of areas. Otherwise, when the next project proposal comes up or a team member wants to bring in new resources, they will not be aware that you want them to produce, for example, a business case to a template.

Similarly with the finance people; if, for the whole ten weeks, you have gone along with the internal reporting systems as they were when you found them, it is going to be more difficult to persuade the finance people to make changes, as it seems to them that you have got along fine for nearly three months since you took the role on.

Interestingly, when Boris Johnson became Mayor of London, he initiated a financial review well within his first ten weeks.

QUICK TIP LOOK FOR QUICK WINS
While you will have to take your time working out your plan for the medium term, always look for opportunities where you and the team can get a fast result. Demonstrate that you are going to make things happen.

What are the potential pitfalls?

At this time you need to find out a lot about the functional side of your role – marketing, engineering or whatever it is. That is probably your main interest and probably the topic that the team will come to you first with questions and requests for decisions. It is easy to forget to work also on the finance and administration side. But you need to understand the relevant company instructions that apply to the team, along with human resources regulations and, of course, the crucial finance side. So, any decision that you make that concerns the main activities of the team will also have a financial dimension, which you must not ignore during the initial phase.

What you need to do is to plan the first ten weeks carefully, taking both sides of the job into account.

What is the worst-case scenario?

Because people often give the benefit of the doubt to those who are starting a new job or joining a new team, things often go well for a period of time. If you make mistakes, they will forgive you because you're new to the job. This is referred to as the 'honeymoon period'. New football coaches, for example, are allowed to lose the first few games without too much criticism. However, after a period of time (the first ten weeks), you, like the coaches, will need to perform well, meeting the expectations of key stakeholders and winning them over as supporters.

During this initial period it is vital that you take the necessary steps to set yourself up for longer-term success. Otherwise you run the risk of falling out of favour: you make a good start but then people begin to see what you are doing as just another management initiative. Plan your first ten weeks carefully in order to set yourself up for longer-term success.

The first ten weeks

What should I do before I start?

If you have the luxury of some time before you take over the new team, and can get access to the internal systems the company uses, then use that time to bone up on how the internal systems work. Find out where you go for human resources information, regulations, health and safety, and so on. Finally, get as good a grasp as you can on the management accounting system.

You are also, of course, gathering information on the functional part of the job. If you are in a finance role, look very carefully at how your new organisation reports performance. Do not assume that all companies are the same, and whatever you do, don't assume that your previous employers were always right.

What do the first ten weeks look like?

Use the following suggestions to put together a plan for the first ten weeks in your new position. We have tried to make it feasible to tackle the financial side in small doses, knowing that you will also be involved in a number of other activities associated with the functional part of the role.

Week 1: Analyse your stakeholders

First impressions will influence the way a relationship develops in the first few months. Start by understanding the key stakeholders in your function area and in the area of finance: what their roles are and how each could impact on your success. These stakeholders will typically include your boss, work colleagues, your team, financial controllers and human resources representatives. Make a list of them and arrange to meet the most significant people – preferably on a one-to-one basis.

Do not go into these initial meetings or telephone conversations without stopping and thinking them through. What is the impression you want to give and what do you need to do to make sure this will happen? Think about what could go wrong and what you can do to ensure risks are avoided or mitigated. Make sure that initial conversations focus on the other people and not you, so take time to really understand what their agenda is, what their concerns are and what their ideas are for the future. Try not to state your ideas at the initial meeting – it is much better just to listen hard. Indeed it is often said that influence most belongs to the person who says least during the meeting but provides the summary at the end and proposes the action plan.

QUICK TIP SEE THE WHOLE PERSON
Don't just concentrate on the organisational role of the person you are meeting for the first time. Find out what makes them tick. Ask them about their family and their hobbies as you try to paint a picture of the whole person.

Week 2: Meet with the financial controller

This person is key. Ask open questions and listen hard to the answers. It is all too easy in these circumstances to misunderstand what they are saying, particularly since they may very well use jargon and because the easiest thing to do is just to sit there and look as though you know what they are talking about. Resist this and ask them over and over again to explain things until you can repeat back to them what they are saying and get their agreement that you have understood correctly.

Set the agenda on three key elements (plus any others that are particular to your situation):

→ **How does the management accounting system work?** Ask what you have to do to make sure that the data you and your team is inputting is accurate. Probe them on what they regard as the weaknesses of the system.

→ **What help can they give in training your people?** They may offer to come and help with financial training or recommend internal or external training mechanisms. In particular, tell them that you regard it as important that everyone understands enough about an annual report to be able to interpret the basic figures from the three main statements: the income statement, balance sheet and cash flow statement.

→ **How are projects evaluated?** Ask them what financial techniques they use: is there a hurdle rate of return; what help will they give the team in presenting business cases; and is there a business template in existence that you could train the team to use?

Do not forget the administration side as well. How do they route contracts (buying or selling) round the organisation to get sign-off; how does the payroll system work; and, if there is one, how is the bonus scheme administered? You will by this time know the areas you need to probe.

If you have a budget for it, take the controller out to lunch. Your gesture could just separate you from the others.

Week 3: Tackle the management accounting system

Now is probably the time to hold a team meeting to discuss the strengths and weaknesses of the management accounting system. Invite the financial controller too. Remember that this meeting should end with agreement on the key places where you are going to press for clarification or for change.

There is more detail on this system, particularly its desired attributes, in Chapter 4.

Week 4: Carry out a team SWOT analysis

You now know enough about the team and they know enough about what you are looking for to carry out a SWOT analysis on all their activities. Get them together and write down a summary of the current position, using sentences rather than bullet points to avoid misunderstandings. You can do this for the team's normal functions and for its skills in the area of finance. Here is the finance side:

→ **Strengths.** What is the team competent at doing? What activities is it really good at?

→ **Weaknesses.** In what areas is the team short of resources or capabilities?

→ **Opportunities.** How can the team boost its financial performance? Where, for example, could training help? Make sure that this list includes your view on the use of annual reports for research and making business cases.

→ **Threats.** What are the financial pitfalls that will occur if the team does not improve its performance?

This will help you to determine what your vision for the future is. What you hope to achieve will emerge from the opportunities; what changes you will have to make will be clear from the weaknesses. By the end of this week you will have an outline of your plan that you can refine and add more detail to a little later on.

QUICK TIP DON'T GET BOGGED DOWN
Ensure that SWOT analysis gives a structure to the discussion and is not a pedantic piece of bureaucracy. If people are arguing whether something is a weakness or a threat, for example, remind them that it does not really matter. As long as the idea is documented, wherever that is, it will have an impact on the team's plan.

Week 5: Carry out a post hoc cost justification of a completed project

Do this with an individual or a subset of the team, preferably those agents of change that you are hoping will help you to get the team to be more financially aware. Perhaps the easiest way of finding the ideal project is to look at an area where the team spent a substantial sum of money. It could be capital expenditure, a training course, an addition to their accommodation or an additional spend with the IT department.

An outline of how to do this can be found in Chapter 3 (page 60, detailing investment appraisal), with more detail given in the Director's Toolkit. Make sure to use the company template if one is available.

Week 6: Train the team on annual reports

By this time you know which annual reports are worth analysing. The team should analyse the accounts of your own company in order to improve their knowledge of the business. It is also useful to analyse the accounts of companies that you deal with or compete against. Make sure that the training you do is based on a computer model that people can use later. If you have this model available on the intranet, you can get them to go through the process during the training course and have access to each other's work. This also means that if they agree to do further analyses after the course, you will be able to monitor their progress – or lack of it.

Week 7: Take a break to reflect

By the end of week 6 you will hopefully have done a great job, but you will also be pretty tired. Even the most capable and confident managers tend to use up a lot of nervous energy when getting stuck into a new job. Try to remain calm and avoid getting stressed.

Use this week to take time to relax and get to know the team better. Spend time with each team member on a one-on-one basis and listen to their views, their aspirations and their concerns. Talk to your key stakeholders and test the various elements of your financial vision, updating it as you go.

Pay particular attention to your boss and try to understand them better. What is their preferred leadership style, what do they think are the major opportunities and threats, and how do they feel your first six weeks have gone?

During this week make sure you get on top of your day-to-day administration and clear as much of your in-box as possible. Ensure that your email list is under control and take time to delegate non-critical tasks to members of the team as early as possible. Remember that it is much better to deal with issues early, before they become crises.

Week 8: Agree the business template

There are two phases to validating a new project or a new way of working – the strategic fit, which is whether the new idea fits well into your team's strategy, and the financial validation or test of return on investment. The business template covers the first part.

To create the template, list the most important criteria of your strategy. One criterion, for example, might be to minimise external subcontractors, while another might be to operate within the current team's resources. Give each criterion a rating out of ten that reflects its importance, with ten being the highest priority. That gives the weighting you will attach to that criterion when you measure new ideas against it. For each criterion define the 'ideal' case. So, for the example of minimising external subcontractors, you may ideally want any new idea to use subcontractors for less than 20% of the work; while in the case of the team, ideally you would add no resources at all.

This gives you the template against which to measure any new idea or project. You will prefer and move on with the projects or proposals that come nearest to the ideal you have created in the template.

Week 9: Work on the first cost-benefit analysis

You have a decision to make now. How are you going to measure the financial return on investment on proposals for the projects, capital expenditure or any new activities that your customers or your team have come up with?

If you decide on any technique that is more complicated than the payback method, you will almost certainly need to train your people in the use of that technique. This is a good opportunity to involve your financial controller, since they will be aware of any company standards that you could apply.

Week 10: Develop a two-year plan

Over the last nine weeks you have built your reputation and credibility in your functional role, you have developed important relationships with influential stakeholders and your confidence has grown. At the same time you have developed your own and your team's knowledge and skills in the finance area. You will by now have an opinion on what you want to achieve based on facts and the advice of experts around the business. Now is the time to develop your two-year plan.

CASE STORY ACCOUNTANCY CONSULTANCY COMPANY, ALAN'S STORY

Narrator Alan is a consultant with a solid background in accountancy.

Context A new managing director at an accountancy consultancy firm had been used to using KPIs to control his previous business. Very quickly he put in place no fewer than eight KPIs for each of the fee earners, simply transferring the system he had used in his old job to the new environment.

Issue This was a wholesale upheaval for team leaders. They spent so much time trying to resolve problems in meeting their KPIs that the new set of management accounts were out before they had properly decided what had happened and what to do.

Solution The finance director realised what was going on. He had been worried about the speed of change in the first place. He called in Alan to analyse the problem. Alan suggested that the team leaders get together with the finance director and the managing director, and agree a more limited number of KPIs as alternative measures. Since the team leaders knew what would work, they were able to introduce KPIs that were manageable and still gave the MD what he wanted.

Learning Don't overdo things in the first ten weeks and make sure you involve others in planning change. If you are a team member in such a situation, like the finance director here, somehow you have got to get the new boss to consult. Although they may be bringing new skills to the business, they cannot know as much as you do about the people who have been there for a while.

A lot will depend on whether you are starting from scratch or taking over an existing team, but in either case start by reflecting on your earlier vision and update it if necessary. Perhaps you can be more ambitious in implementing the financial framework you will operate within. Then work back and identify what needs to be done and achieved on a month-by-month basis. Keep the plan for year 2 at a high level, but plan the first three months in detail.

Once you have your plan, identify barriers or potential problems that could get in your way. What could go wrong, what could cause this to happen and what can you do to prevent it? Build these actions into the plan.

Finally, you should be as specific as possible about how you will know if you are succeeding. Set key performance indicators that you can monitor on a monthly basis that will let you and your boss know whether you are on track. Make sure that at least one indicator tracks the financial benefits of your work, as this will help you to justify future investment in you and your team.

QUICK TIP WORK TO A PLAN
Get the team involved in building your plan, from SWOT analysis to evaluating alternatives. The more they contribute to the plan, the more seriously they will take it.

Checklist: what do I need to know?

During your first ten weeks in a new job, start gathering information that will help you to deliver results, build your team and develop your career. Use the following checklist to see if you have the necessary information – using a simple Red-Amber-Green status, where Red reflects major gaps in current knowledge and suggests immediate action is required, and Amber suggests some knowledge is missing and may need to be addressed at some stage in the future. Green means you are happy with the current state.

TOPIC	INFORMATION	RAG
Business context	The major trends in the industry that will impact what you do, how you do it and your priorities	
Business strategy	The overall strategy for the business in terms of its products and markets and the basis on which it differentiates itself in the market	
Team objectives	The key performance indicators (KPIs) that will be used to assess whether you and your team have been a success	
Stakeholders	Those individuals or groups that you will work with and that will influence success or failure of your innovation activities	
The team	Individual members of your team – their names, their backgrounds and their relative strengths and weaknesses	
Roles	The defined roles and responsibilities needed to deliver results – internal to the team or external contributors	
Customers	Your top five internal or external customers and their specific musts and wants	
Suppliers	Your top ten suppliers – who they are and how they contribute to the success of your team	
Your boss	Your operational manager – who they are, their preferred style and what it is that really makes them tick	
The director	The person leading your activities within the business, and possibly the person whose job you aspire to	
Key opinion leaders	People across the organisation whose expert knowledge and opinion is respected by others – who they are and what they each have to offer	
Current commitments	The current operational team activities – what they are and what it will take to make them succeed	
Future workload	Future expectations in terms of what needs to be delivered when and by whom	
Budget	The amount of funding available for your activities – where this will come from and what the sign-off process is	
Resources	The people, facilities, equipment, materials and information available to you for your activities	
Scope	The boundaries that have been set for you and your team – the things you are not allowed to do	
Key events	The major events that are happening within the business that will influence what you need to do and when	

TOPIC	INFORMATION	RAG
Potential problems	The risks you face going forward – the things that could go wrong based on the assumptions you have made	☐
SWOT	The relative strengths, weaknesses, opportunities and threats for your team	☐
Review process	The formal review process for your internal team reviews, at which KPIs will be reviewed with your boss	☐

STOP – THINK – ACT

Now put together a plan for your first ten weeks.

What should I do?	What do I need to achieve?
Who do I need to involve?	Who needs to be involved and why?
What resources will I require?	What information, facilities, materials, equipment or budget will be required?
What is the timing?	When will tasks be achieved?
	Week 1
	Week 2
	Week 3
	Week 4
	Week 5
	Week 6
	Week 7
	Week 8
	Week 9
	Week 10

Visit **www.Fast-Track-Me.com** to use the Fast Track online planning tool.

EXPERT VOICE

Value drivers of corporate deals

Dr Giampiero Favato

On 1 February 2008 Microsoft Corp. offered to buy Yahoo Inc. for $44.6 billion, in a bold bid to transform two ailing internet businesses into a worthy competitor for market leader Google Inc. In what would be the biggest internet deal since the ill-fated Time Warner–AOL merger, Microsoft offered $31 per Yahoo share, in cash and stock. The price was a 62% premium over Yahoo's same-day close, but only about a quarter of what the internet company was worth at the height of the dotcom bubble in 2000.

Investors applauded Microsoft's bid, sending shares of Yahoo up nearly 50% during the next day's trading. But the backdrop of the news was an internet advertising market that had significant potential for growth yet still faced some uncertainty. Google reported fourth-quarter earnings that failed to meet Wall Street expectations.[1]

Some analysts said Microsoft was overpaying for a company that had warned earlier in the week that it had faced 'head winds' in 2008, forecasting revenue below Wall Street expectations. Global Equities Research analyst Trip Chowdhry said Yahoo was not worth more than $20 per share, since its only worthwhile properties were Yahoo Mail, Yahoo Answers and Yahoo Finance.[2]

On 14 February Yahoo formally declined Microsoft's offer, as the bid substantially undervalued the company as a whole.

Was the Microsoft bid too high or too low?

The result of an acquisition can be measured as increased cash flows for the newly combined business, as compared to the sum of the cash flows of the two pre-acquisition firms. The value of a company can be shown to depend on the perspective taken. The same company in the hands of another owner may be able to create substantially more value.

How is value added from a merger or acquisition? Potential synergies may result, the benefits of which can be related to their impact on the value drivers of the shareholder value analysis approach.[3] For example:

→ Sales growth may improve because of being able to use the distribution channels of each organisation to sell the products of both.

[1] Walters, R. (2008), 'Microsoft challenges Google's grip', *FT Weekend*, 2–3 February, 8.
[2] Ordohez, J. and Braiker, B. (2008), 'Is Yahoo worth $44.6 billion? Microsoft is paying a premium to catch up to Google', *Newsweek*, 1 February, available at **www.newsweek.com/id/107020**
[3] Mills, R.W. (2007), *Corporate Finance: A Managerial Perspective*, The Hague, Netherlands: Value Focus.

→ Increases in operating profit margins may be possible because of being able to use production facilities more efficiently.

→ Cash taxes may be saved by being able to plan the tax position of the new combined organisation. This area may be particularly beneficial for certain types of cross-border deal.

→ The total level of capital invested can be decreased. Fixed capital requirements may be lowered by being able to use available spare capacity for increased sales activity. There may also be an impact on replacement capital requirements. A good example of this is a decision to merge by two high street clearing banks: it may be possible to provide service to both sets of customers in the new organisation while cutting the number of branches.

→ Working capital requirements can be reduced if the two businesses have a profile of cash flows opposite in effect to one another. There may also be potential benefits arising from better debtor, creditor and stock management.

→ The planning period may be lengthened because, for example, the new larger venture increases barriers to entry.

→ The cost of capital may fall if access is obtained to cheaper sources of finance.

→ Furthermore, the discounted cash flow framework can be applied by valuing the acquired and target companies on a standalone basis and then comparing the sum of the two values obtained with their estimated value as a combined entity, making due allowance for all potential synergistic benefits. To be meaningful in managerial terms, such valuations require the identification of the key value drivers so that the potential sources of benefit can be understood and analysed.

LEADING THE TEAM

Leadership is as important to success as gaining expert knowledge and being familiar with appropriate tools and techniques. Focus on your personal attributes as a leader and reflect on what it takes to lead and develop a team.

Changing myself

The ultimate test of leadership is the top job. As you progress in that direction you need the people above you and the people below you to admire the way you go about leading your team. Good senior managers can smell a well-motivated happy team from a mile off. The team members exude confidence. They work hard and make sacrifices. They display pride in their work and in their membership of what they honestly believe is the best bit of the organisation. Not only that, but everyone, including human resources, will know that people are queuing up to get into that team. All this is good for your career. So, how do you create this aura for the top folk to sniff?

> **QUICK TIP TREAT SENIOR MANAGERS WELL**
> While in no way encouraging sycophancy, it is worth remembering that senior managers are as vain as anyone and vainer than most. If they visit your team then treat them properly: posh black cars to pick them up at the airport, unusual as well as expensive hotels, and so on. They may preach hair shirt but they may not wear them. This is almost certainly one time that you do not economise.

There are arguments that say that leaders are born and cannot be created, and it is true that your basic ability to get on with people is, to some extent, your starting point for being a leader. But there are some techniques in leadership that develop your natural ability to make things happen. Think about motivation – leadership is the skill of persuading people to cooperate willingly to achieve results. Willingly is key; you cannot force motivation on people – they have to want to do a good job. Motivation occurs when people feel that they are able to make their very best contribution.

What personal attributes will I need?

The starting point for managing an effective team is to manage yourself. Too often managers are good at setting career and personal development activities for members of their team, but are less diligent with their own personal development planning.

Conducting a self-assessment against four dimensions is a useful starting point. Do you have the necessary **knowledge** to do the job? What about skills and **competencies**? Do your **attitudes** and **behaviours** demonstrate your leadership qualities? Use a structured approach to identify specific areas in each of the four categories that you need to work on. However, before taking action, take time to discuss your thoughts with your boss or your coach. Perhaps summarise your thoughts in the form of a SWOT (strengths, weaknesses, opportunities and threats) before putting a plan together. However, do not be over-ambitious and try to develop yourself too quickly – becoming an effective leader takes time.

In terms of finance, show a commitment and a positive attitude to getting the finance side right. Whether the objective is to make profits or to stay within a budget and improve services at the same time, you need to demonstrate that the finance side is key. Read the financial pages of a newspaper and discuss relevant issues with the team. Treat the organisation's money as though it were your own and you will be surprised how the team starts to do the same. Never cut corners or cheat. Nothing makes a leader look smaller than exploiting the expenses system – travelling second class and claiming first is a good example of the sort of petty mindedness that will harm your reputation.

What leadership style is appropriate?

Do you tell 'em or sell 'em? Some people talk about 'push' and 'pull' management styles. Push is the 'Do what you are told' or autocratic method; pull is the consulting, democratic way of leading people. You need a combination of the two for different people and in different situations.

So, leadership of a team is on a style continuum that ranges from simple directives to group discussion and consensus. Remember that if you veer too much towards giving directions you will, among other things, stifle the creativity of the team. That in turn reduces the number of times you will be able to take a good new idea to your boss. There is almost nothing that boosts a career more than being the first to make an innovative idea work and having it taken up by the rest of the company. Everybody will want to talk to you about it, to find out how to follow your lead.

Always remember that people work for money but do a bit extra for recognition, praise and reward. If you think someone is doing a good job, don't forget to tell them. Show appreciation often. Don't wait for the end of a task to say 'Thanks'. It is often a good idea to thank someone in the middle of a project for getting on with it without you having to take time to be involved. Show a genuine interest in other people, communicate well and pick the right style at the right time and you, too, can become a born leader.

There is a great opportunity to combine a consensual style of leadership with a key financial process, and that is the annual budgeting cycle. So, as well as involving the team in agreeing your strategy and the action plans you will implement to achieve that strategy, involve the team in setting the budget. You may need to hold a meeting on this topic alone or add the budget in as an agenda item to a planning meeting. If you do it openly and show that you appreciate their contribution to the budget, you will find that they will volunteer areas where savings could be made, where services could be improved for no extra cost and where revenue can be improved.

QUICK TIP DON'T CAP BONUS BUDGETS
If you include in the budget bonuses for strong performance, then don't cap them. If someone overperforms to such an extent that the payment is very large, congratulate them and pay up.

Motivating the individual

It is not uncommon for a new team leader to be faced with a team that has low morale. The team needs a new leader, perhaps because the old one did not get them to perform to their best or achieve their objectives. In this instance the new leader faces more than the normal problems of taking on a new team – the wariness of a team that doesn't know them and so on. The new leader has also got to 'get their heads back up'. Whether or not this is the case, recognise the importance of spending a huge amount of time with the team, talking to them and getting to know them.

Low motivation and morale frequently start from a simple communications problem. The team does not feel that management is being open with them or keeping them informed of what is going on. This often happens when a manager is trying not to worry a team with problems affecting the organisation. This never works; the team members are not fools and they know something is going on, so they worry, even though they do not have the details of what to worry about. So make sure as quickly as you can that they hear the full story of the organisation's position and the impact on them.

The other main cause of team demotivation is their lack of involvement with the decision-making process. They feel as though their view is not taken into account when plans are being made. If this is true, they are quite right to feel bad about it. The best people to find a way round problems or improve a difficult situation are almost always the people at the coalface. If you want to know how to sell more products and services, ask the salespeople. If you need to reduce direct costs, ask the people in production, and so on. Use a structured, but quite simple team-planning process that makes certain that everyone contributes to planning the way ahead.

But how do you keep your team wanting to come to work in the morning, for ever? Giving them responsibility is key. For example, assigning teams of, say, two people to find solutions to issues tends to work well and produces solutions quickly. It is stronger than each individual working on their own with occasional input from their leader. It is also important for a team to have a wide perspective of what is going on in the organisation. Making absolutely sure that they know how important they and their work are to the whole organisation is a huge motivator. You can make it work even better if you translate their achievements into financial terms. If the team's job is to provide services but not at a profit, then have some measure in place that compares their performance with others to show that they are giving really good value for money. In a profit-making organisation you need to be able to demonstrate what contribution they are making to the overall organisation. It is this concentration on relating back to the financial side that develops the finance-aware culture that leads to financial success.

QUICK TIP TEAM TARGETS
By all means set a team target so that a bonus is paid to everyone for the team's success, but balance it with individual targets, so that one person can be rewarded for their individual efforts as well.

Bonuses and rewards are part of motivating the members of a team but by no means the whole of it. Understand the crucial importance of appreciating their efforts – they need regular praise and thanks for the efforts they are putting in. Sometimes it is good to set monthly goals so that the team can get together more frequently to celebrate their achievements. Finally, people need to get involved in new activities and new challenges on a regular basis.

Building the team

What makes a great team?

So, you have a great leadership style that is flexible enough to cope with different situations, and you have a number of highly motivated and skilled people to work with – but that does not necessarily make them a great team. So what do the successful teams do that differentiates them from average performers? Read through the following checklist and reflect on what you need to do as leader of the team in order to ensure success.

→ **The team will have great clarity in its goals and have a real sense of purpose.** Fast Track teams will have such clarity of vision that they will know how they want to be remembered long after they have been disbanded. For example, a team-planning session can potentially be remembered as the time when the team developed the new ideas that transformed not only their part of the business but also the company's fortunes.

→ **The team will have a strong and enthusiastic leader who provides direction, is supportive of team members and is willing to shoulder responsibility when things do not go according to plan.** The leader is often not the expert or specialist but understands how to bring experts together and get them to perform effectively as a unit.

→ **Fast Track teams also accept that things will change and can act flexibly in order to bring things back on track.** Perhaps a team is implementing a major change programme, like developing a business case template, and within the first week a key member of the team leaves. They will reappraise the situation quickly but calmly, explore creative options for dealing with the situation and move on.

→ **They will have shared values and a common set of operating principles.** While teams comprise people with a variety of skills and experiences, they need to be unified by common beliefs. We see the enormous power that the adoption of a common set of religious beliefs can have for both positive and negative ends, and while levels of fanaticism are rarely positive, shared values will often provide the team with enormous energy and commitment.

→ **Ideally, the shared values then extend into a general respect and liking for each other, where members of the team trust each other and genuinely have fun working together.** Encourage them to get together for recreation outside working hours, but beware of two pitfalls in this. The first is that the team becomes too insular and does not make cross-functional contacts by joining in with other organisation-wide initiatives. The second pitfall is that some people simply do not want to have the same people as friends and work mates. Respect that view.

→ **There will be issues to deal with, but the Fast Track teams will manage these quickly and sensitively before they become crises.** To do this they need to have open and honest communication and work in a blame-free environment.

→ **While these teams will focus on their primary objectives, they will have a feeling of shared responsibility and be supportive of each other.** They will take time out to learn and develop new skills – both individually and as a team. This necessitates keeping an eye on how they are performing and scanning other similar teams in order to identify alternative approaches that could be adopted.

→ **The team will be balanced in terms of the skills and capabilities of team members and in terms of the roles they each fulfil.** The team will have people capable of creative challenge, but it also needs people willing to get their heads down in order to put the work in and deliver the results.

How should I develop the team?

Take the formal side of developing the team very seriously. Prepare thoroughly for appraisals and get team members to do that too. Make sure that each of them has some sort of personal development plan. Use the formal organisation-wide development plan if one exists, and write the plan down if it doesn't. Where training is required, fight hard to get it and never let a crisis prevent someone going on a planned training course. Remember that net exporters of managers tend to have higher-flying careers than those who keep their people for long periods of time. If you develop your team well, other managers will steal them. This is a nuisance in the short term but in the long term it pays off. Ambitious people will see you as a good person to work for and you will get people queuing up to join your team.

QUICK TIP LIFE GOES ON
Don't hang on to people at all costs. When a premier league football team sells its best player, things do not remain the same – the team regroups and finds the best way of working without that star. It's the same with commercial teams.

Develop the right team members. Some members of your team will come up with more helpful ideas than others – fact. Make sure you are working with the helpful members rather than with your poorer performers. It is much better to spend time with the bulk of your team – the satisfactory performers – and try to get their average performance up. It is, after all, the satisfactory performers and high-flyers who will come up with the best suggestions. If you spend your time training and coaching them, preparing tools to help with productivity and showing them exemplars of how to perform better, you may raise their average by a significant percentage. This improvement is spread across the majority of the team and so your overall performance will take a big jump.

Then get them rather than you to present new thoughts to your boss and higher up. Their enthusiasm will shine through and you will be seen as a great leader.

But what do you do with your low performers? This is a tough question, particularly if it is impossible or undesirable to fire them. The answer is also tough. Give them a strictly limited amount of your time. At best they will get the message and move on. At worst they will move on, criticising you for being unhelpful. You will have covered yourself in advance for this latter response by explaining what you are doing to your boss. And if they are spending too much time with their no-hopers, they could be very grateful for your help.

Look at the issue financially. Suppose you have a team of twelve. Two of them are high-flyers and need little help to produce £100,000 in profits each year. Eight are satisfactory and produce on average £80,000. The two back-markers each produce £40,000. Let's say that spending a lot of time and resources with the poor performers improves their productivity by 25%, which is a net gain to the team performance of £20,000. If you spread the same time and resources among the eight satisfactory performers, let's say you would improve their productivity by 10%. That's a gain of £64,000. QED, develop those with potential rather than trying to redeem the irredeemable.

CASE STORY COMPUTER HARDWARE COMPANY, KEN'S STORY

Narrator Ken is a first-line sales manager for a major computer hardware company.

Context This is a very fast-moving business and new products must sell quickly because the competition will soon catch up. To get a good launch of a new product, Ken decided to delegate to the salespeople the decision to offer a 10% reduction in price in return for quick decisions from their customers.

Issue In fact the salespeople, wanting a quick and easy win, mistimed the offer by putting the discounted price in as the first proposal. So, whether customers ordered quickly or not, it was impossible to get back up to the list price. This meant that the company was going to miss its projected profit on the new product by a fair margin.

Solution Ken removed the delegated power and put the team leaders in charge of discounting.

Learning When you are delegating, think about how a person under pressure might create an unforeseen consequence. Particularly when you are dealing with customers, internal or external, remember to keep control of the profitability of deals while delegating other parts of the sales process.

STOP – THINK – ACT

Reflect on how well you are leading the team and look for ways you could improve. Think about how well the team is operating and how committed each member of the team is.

What should we do?	What actions do we need to take to build the team?
Who do we need to involve?	Who needs to be involved and why?
What resources will we require?	What level of investment would be required?
What is the timing?	What deadlines do we need to meet?

Visit **www.Fast-Track-Me.com** to use the Fast Track online planning tool.

ABCD quality based costing

Keith Baxter

EXPERT VOICE

Applying risk management to an ongoing programme to 'rescue it' is quite common. But the problem is that the programme has already gone wrong, and this is often due to the fact that the estimating assumptions made when the project was in the scoping/proposal stage were fundamentally incorrect. This often leads to insufficient budgets, shortcuts and damaged business relationships that ultimately undermine the project, leading to delays, scoping reductions and even total project failure.

So what's wrong with traditional estimating techniques?

Traditional estimating approaches take 'good quality' estimates (e.g. capital assets) and 'poor quality' estimates (e.g. resource estimates for activities never attempted before) and simply add them together to produce an 'add-up cost' that conceals the uncertainties. Further, if these uncertainties are now lost in the add-up cost there is no way of re-analysing and therefore no way of managing the cost-risk by directly addressing the uncertainty risks.

What can be done to improve this?

Quality based costing (QBC)[1] is a proven way of accurately estimating the cost-risk (i.e. the budget, timescales and/or benefits) in any size of programme. It essentially works by acknowledging the inevitable quality variations in the estimates and underpins all estimates with their underlying assumptions.

So how does quality based costing work?

QBC uses the concept of first identifying the strategic cost 'bricks' in the project. The term brick is simply used to avoid confusion with work packages, activities, tasks, etc., and the size of a brick can vary considerably depending on the stage of the project. The first step is to build the 'brick wall', and when this is complete, the total cost structure of the project is represented (with no estimates at this stage).

Brick owners are allocated for each brick, based on the ability to estimate the specific brick as accurately as possible. Brick owners are then interviewed to 'break down' the brick estimates into its components.

This is done by asking structured questions that break the brick down into:

A	**A**bsolute minimum
A + B	**B**est guess/realistic estimate
A + B + C	**C**ontingency added
A + B + C + D	**D**isaster scenario

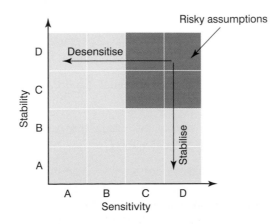

---

[1] Baxter, K. ABCD Quality Based Costing White Paper, available at **www.De-Risk.com** last accessed on 12/3/09, and Baxter, K. (2006), CFO Summit Conference White Paper.

The assumptions that underpin the estimates are also captured using the ABCD assumption analysis process. The key factor here is that the ratings of the assumptions must be consistent with the estimate breakdown. The interview often results in challenges to the estimates and/or assumptions to make them consistent.

Each brick then has two probability distributions built around the estimates – one for the 'contingency scenario' and one for the 'disaster scenario', as shown in the figure below.

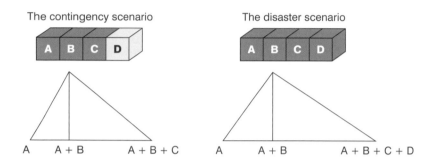

Monte Carlo simulations are then run to statistically add the brick estimates together. The resulting probability distributions can be interpreted to make crucial decisions relating to budgeting, pricing or milestones. For example:

→ There is a zero probability of the project costing less than the base cost.

→ The 50% confidence cost means that there is an 50/50 chance of the project costing less or more than this value.

→ The 90% confidence cost is normally considered to be the 'ideal' cost to budget (if this is considered affordable!).

→ To be meaningful, the project must be funded somewhere between the 50% and 90% costs.

→ The add-up cost is simply the value that would have been reached through traditional estimating.

→ The add-up cost could appear anywhere on the graph (see the next page) but normally appears below the 50% point – is it therefore not surprising that traditional estimating is so far out!

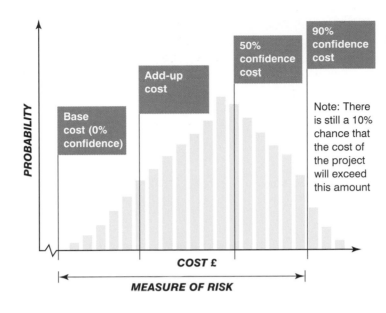

Using QBC for competitive advantage

QBC is often used at the proposal stage of a project to provide the best possible information for competitive pricing and to give confidence that crucial milestones will be met. In non-competitive environments it provides a scientific way of guaranteeing fair budgets and profit. In competitive situations it allows suppliers to understand the level of risk that they are taking on if they choose to cut their price or timescales for strategic reasons. However, it also allows for innovative pricing scenarios which can produce the most aggressive (fixed) price but with reduced risk to the supplier.

8

GETTING TO THE TOP

Finally, think about what you need to do to stand out among your peers, stay up to date and then get ahead. As you progress up the corporate ladder you need to focus continuously on performance, and increasingly look up and out as opposed to in and down. Your network will be more and more important, and you will need to start to think and act like a director.

Your new financial acumen should stand you in good stead amongst your peers. With luck they will be concentrating so hard on getting their work function role right that they will let the finance and administration side slide.

QUICK TIP PURSUE YOUR CAREER
Adopt a positive but sceptical attitude towards your organisation. Don't expect to spend your whole career in one organisation.

Focus on performance

People who perform well and produce good results do tend to get promoted and make it to the top. As well as your normal search for improvement, do a financial audit of your operation from time to time to make sure not only that your performance is above the normal line of duty but also that you can prove that it is. Make a list of all the hard and soft data you use to monitor your performance and do at least a two-year comparison, looking for trends as well as actual increases and reductions.

If you are a profit centre, the data will start from the sales you have made to customers. Use a variation of the product/market matrix we introduced in Chapter 3. This time instead of markets as the top heading use actual customers.

	CUSTOMER A	CUSTOMER B	CUSTOMER C
Product 1 sales value	Year 1: Year 2:	Year 1: Year 2:	Year 1: Year 2:
Product 2 sales value	Year 1: Year 2:	Year 1: Year 2:	Year 1: Year 2:

If, for example, you are an IT team selling hardware and software to all the departments at head office, such an analysis can reveal new opportunities. Why does the sales director spend so little on IT? Look at the trends: who is using you more and who less? Could you use the business case one department made for spend with you as a sales aid to get another department to take the same service? Remember that in the case of software you can sell the same product to the second customer at a very high margin indeed.

CASE STORY SALESMAN TO LOCAL GOVERNMENT, GRAHAM'S STORY

Narrator Graham is a salesperson for an IT company. His patch includes all the local authorities in his area.

Context All local governments are ruled by the same legislation and are trying to solve the same problem – offering good services to council-tax payers and keeping council tax under control.

Issue By doing a detailed analysis of what his local government invested in technology, Graham noticed that one institution was spending much less and using technology in a less adventurous way than any of his other customers.

Solution Graham persuaded the chief executive to allow him and the IT department to look at areas where technology was little used. They found, among other things, that there was a senior engineer in the roads department who was nearing retirement and very unwilling to introduce anything new into the department. The chief executive moved the man sideways, put a more dynamic person in charge and soon the department started to see the benefits of greater technology investment.

Learning Believe your good logical research and take action.

Now look at your costs in detail. If you run a non-profit making team this is where you will start this exercise. Make a comprehensive list of where you spend actual money – money going out of the company – and where you spend virtual money – money transferred to another team's profit and loss account. Check that internal suppliers are giving you good value for money by getting an outside agency to quote to do the same job. Look at two-year spending and find the trends. Look too at your soft measures – those items that are not financial but are measurable, like activity levels, or items that are less easy to measure, such as quality.

Use your team. Remember that by now you have their attitude right and they are spending company money as though it were their own. This means they will help, if you show them the trends, to find areas where pain-free savings can be made. Note the words 'pain free': your hair-shirt routines do not mean that your team is badly paid or getting a raw deal on expenses and company-backed Christmas parties, but they do mean that unnecessary expense is rooted out and checked from time to time. Sometimes, for example, an internal cost is maintained where the service has become unnecessary – get rid of it.

Let's finish this section by giving one more illustration of the difference between the sort of person whose attitude to finance gets them to the top and middle managers who never really get the point.

Ken, working as an independent consultant, asked some senior people from his customers to come to a Test match. He supplied their ticket, lunch and wine with lunch – not madly expensive, but not cheap either. A sales manager from one of his clients did not turn up to take his seat. He did not make contact; he simply did not arrive. Ken phoned him and found that something had cropped up a couple of days before that had stopped him coming and he had forgotten to let Ken know. The sales manager was quite matter of fact about the whole thing, but when Ken explained what had happened to a production director who was at the match, the man was shocked. He was really shocked that someone could behave like that. The director understood; the sales manager just didn't get it.

Invite challenge

Who can we get to challenge us?

If you want to get to the top you can never rest on your laurels. You may think that your performance is on track, but as the external business environment changes you need to adapt. Look for ways to introduce challenge to you and your team on a regular basis, aiming to bring in ideas, tools and techniques from recognised leaders in good practice. Review different groups:

→ **Other internal teams.** What ideas can be shared? What common risks can be avoided? How do they organise their management accounts? Do they use other soft measures of performance, such as activity monitoring?

→ **Customers.** How are their must-haves, needs and wants changing? What future scenarios might occur? Is there some way you can add value to what you supply to them that will enable you to increase your price?

→ **Competitors.** What are they doing now that could be copied ('swiped')?

→ **Supply chain.** What possibilities are there for improved effectiveness and efficiency? What are you still doing the old way because you and the team have never challenged the methodology?

→ **Industry advisers.** What are the experts recommending? Which way is the economy going and what impact will it have on you?

Even if you are meeting your key performance indicators, take on challenging acts on a regular basis so that you are ahead of the game. If you are finding it easy to meet the targets set for you, then don't wait for your boss to make them more stretching – do it yourself. Perhaps take time to get involved in areas where you are not confident in order to continuously develop yourself.

Remember to use relevant opportunities for self-development and self-promotion both inside and outside work, within your function and without. For example:

→ Always volunteer to speak at internal training courses. This brings you into contact with a lot of people, particularly if it means going to a training centre that senior people go to.

→ Get involved in an outside body concerned with strategic issues relating to your function or to finance. Something that keeps you up to date with the local business scene can be especially useful.

→ Get on to the steering committee of a professional institute.

→ Respond to public inquires (from the government) and try to get on review bodies by developing a reputation for being a willing volunteer.

→ Get experience of board work through acting in the role in a company spin-out, or increase your exposure to your own company board and their way of thinking by making presentations when the opportunity arises.

→ Get on internal working parties investigating company issues outside your area and preferably with a big financial element.

How do I keep up to date?

You need talent, artistry, political awareness and opportunism to enjoy the best your career can offer. You also need knowledge. This knowledge is much wider than your own industry.

Read external sources widely on and around your subject. In our research to find out what makes great businesspeople tick, we asked a director of a large company what made the managing director so successful. (He is now a knight of the realm and a confidant of an ex-prime minister.) We had met the MD and knew him to be very clever and very quick. What else was there to him? 'I'm not sure,' said the director, 'but I do know that he is in his office every evening until about 9.30.' 'What on earth is he doing?' we asked. 'Well, reading mainly. He keeps up to date with everything there is to read about the business climate, his industry and his customer's industry.'

QUICK TIP IT'S UP TO YOU
It is old-fashioned and rather naïve to expect your boss and the human resources department to look after your career. Think about your career yourself – plan and make it happen by your own efforts.

Sir Peter Walters, ex-chairman of BP and SmithKline Beecham, put it this way:

> Looking back on my own career I think the one thing that perhaps helped me was the breadth of my reading about the oil industry and overall economic matters. In addition, of course, to being up to speed in the depth of knowledge to do the job of the moment. Perhaps it helped that I was an economist and had an interest in reading as widely as possible; and indeed the whole subject of economics is one where at the time of taking my original degree the macro rather than the micro was the area of discussion and debate. Perhaps this only means that to get on in life you have to be someone of whom it cannot be said 'He or she cannot see the wood for the trees'.

Getting promoted

Getting to the top is a political exercise as well as a matter of carrying out your job effectively. Look for ways that you can increase your internal contacts high and wide. Getting promoted to a high level needs work and dedication. Your move into first-line management was probably not that difficult – people need to fill jobs and anyone who stands even a bit out in the crowd will tend to be noticed and promoted. But at second-line level and certainly above that it gets much more difficult. After all, by definition the chaff has been weeded out and the competition you are now against are all people who are recognised as being good. Make a plan of things to do that will ensure you again stand out in a much more able crowd.

Here are a couple of ideas.

Put up a paper

At any point in the chaos that describes your organisation, there can come an opportunity for you to make a sensible suggestion, which, if good enough, could make your star shine. Be continuously on the look-out. Perhaps there is a product feature kept too long to be competitive, a business process that reflects how things were some time ago, an opportunity for using technology that will make a significant contribution to the effectiveness of the organisation, a cost that could be reduced or revenue that could be increased. Other possibilities may be in the area of publicity or sponsorship. For example, if you know the arts or sport preferences of the chief executive, you might just stumble across a local opportunity for sponsorship. If you pull it off, you can be sure the chief executive will be there for the event.

First make sure that your idea is in an area where the issues are being discussed at least two levels above you, which is your target audience. These are not the specific issues of your idea but are related. Now put up a paper.

Keep it brief, simple and in their terms. Use a formula like this:

→ **Scope of the paper:** showing the areas covered.

→ **Background:** showing what you have done to get to this point.

→ **Problem or opportunity:** expressed in their terms.

→ **Basis of decision:** outlining how they should judge your solution.

→ **Solution:** make this very specific.

→ **Benefits to the organisation:** including what is in it for them, the report readers.

→ **Future plan of action.**

Once you have written the paper, try to shorten it significantly, say by half. Throw out anything except the essentials. Remember that you want to have the opportunity to discuss it, so if it is too comprehensive you may have given everything lock, stock and barrel to someone else to dine out on. Release it effectively. This means in the way that best serves your interests. After all, it was your idea.

A good paper may help in other ways as well. There are lots of conferences out there, and lots of organisers looking for people to read papers to them. Try to find one inside or outside your organisation. Remember that reading a paper anywhere abroad looks very good on your CV.

Abolish your job and create a new one

Abolishing your job may seem a risky thing to do, but it is a great mistake in career planning to assume that the current management structure is the one in which you have to succeed. Indeed, the opposite is the case.

Many jobs exist because they have always done so, rather than because they represent the best way of doing things. If someone goes into the job and does things the right way, they are probably going outside the original job description that set the post up in the first place. This changed way of operating gets results, but when the person who made the change leaves, their boss will have to change the structure and job description so that the new post consolidates the new way of working. The lesson here is to use your influence and authority to get the best results possible without paying too much attention to how things were done in the past.

QUICK TIP KEEP MOVING JUST TO STAND STILL
Organisations in their natural state ossify. Constantly look for change and avoid losing out to organisations whose management are seeking change.

The corollary of abolishing your job is creating a new one. Managers who succeed are the ones who help the organisation keep up to date and who help to prevent it ossifying.

It is easier to create a new job if the change will help the organisation achieve its objectives better, but it is also possible to do it for your own purposes alone. Possibly starting from putting up a paper, the creation of a new job involves two stages. First, formulate the changed way of doing business that will ensure that the job will exist. Sell this first. That is, show what the changes will do in business and financial terms rather than in structural or people terms. Your case is strongest if you have done a proper return on investment calculation, looking at the costs saved by the new idea and the results gained (notice how once again the ability to do investment appraisal and make business cases comes in handy). If you reveal your hand at this stage there is a good chance that you are mistiming it by being too early. Don't give anyone the opportunity to say that what you are doing is for your own greater glory rather than the advancement of the organisation.

Having sold and got agreement to the requirement for change, produce your implementation plan and, of course, include the new positions required. Do not at this stage play any kind of shrinking violet game; clearly show that you are the person for the role you have both chosen and defined. You have the business case behind you and it has been agreed, so tell people that you should have the job. Make sure the new job description has all the elements needed for the next step – access to senior management and a high profile when required. The risk and return on this career procedure will be very good if you have got it right. After all, you have moulded a job where the circumstances and your skills will be a perfect fit.

The message here is clear – plan your career in the same way as you plan every other activity in your work life.

Becoming a director

What does a manager do?

The easiest way to understand what a director does is to start from the basics of what a manager does. We can then look at the differences at board level.

→ Managers are there to enable their people to give of their best.

→ They are effective implementers of corporate and divisional strategy. They are always able to connect their activities with the bigger picture.

→ As well as implementing it, they have a role in influencing high-level strategy. First-line managers are the voice of their people, markets and suppliers. They see the changes day to day and are in the best position to question or suggest alterations to the way the organisation goes about its affairs.

→ Managers are a skilled resource to their team. They must add value when they are in action, helping the team. For instance, when a sales manager goes to see a customer, the plan for the meeting must make them do or say something that could not be done or said by the team member. Another good example is when a production manager visits a supplier and introduces environmental issues.

→ Managers know how the organisation works and can thus add to the efficiency and productivity of their team.

QUICK TIP VALUE THE PACKAGE CORRECTLY
If you are offered shares in an unquoted small business as an inducement to join the board, value them at zero as you evaluate the whole package. Despite what the current owners tell you, in most cases that will still be their value in many years' time.

What does a director do that is different?

So, what do you add or change when you become a director? You are the member of the executive team committed to driving the whole function – sales, production or whatever – forward. Whatever the function and title, the director will fulfil various roles in addition to meeting their statutory responsibilities. These include:

→ setting the overall functional strategy and gaining the active support of the chief executive and other members of the board;

→ championing their function so that sufficient budget and resources are assigned to its activities across the organisation in the face of competition from other operating divisions and other functions;

→ ensuring members of the board are aware of critical trends in technology and the marketplace, the impact of each on business performance and the implications in terms of driving fundamental change;

→ designing the overall management framework for the directorate and putting in place the appropriate teams and champions to ensure effective implementation;

→ reporting on your function's progress and performance to the board, conducting stakeholder presentations and briefing key opinion leaders inside and outside the organisation.

What will my statutory responsibilities be?

As well as heading up the functional activities throughout the business, you will have certain roles and statutory responsibilities that accompany the title of director. As a member of the board of directors, you will be involved in:

→ determining the company's strategic objectives and policies;

→ monitoring progress towards achieving the objectives and policies;

→ appointing the senior management team;

→ accounting for the company's activities to relevant parties, e.g. shareholders;

→ attending board meetings that run the company, with the high level of integrity that is inferred by statutory standards and the company's interpretation of corporate governance, particularly in sensitive areas such as health and safety.

You will also have to conduct yourself in a highly professional manner.

→ A director must not put themselves in a position where the interests of the company conflict with their personal interests or duties to third parties.

→ A director must not make a personal profit out of their position as a director unless they are permitted to do so by the company.

→ A director must act bona fide in what they consider is in the interests of the company as a whole, and not for any other purpose and with no other agenda.

Planning your exit strategy

How long do you want to be in each job before seeking your next promotion? As we saw in Chapter 6, it takes about ten weeks to take stock of the new job, set the new direction and start the process of implementing your strategy and plan. You probably need to give it a year to demonstrate any success; so after a year and ten weeks, the time has come to sniff around for a new job.

This is why you need to plan an exit strategy. You want to be indispensable to the organisation but not to the job you are doing at the moment. You do not want to be the victim of senior people saying that they need you to stay put because you are getting good results in an area that is important to the organisation. Identify as quickly as you can at least one person and preferably two, who you will groom to take your job over. To do this, always recruit the best people you can attract. It's much better to have someone who really wants your job than to play safe and recruit people who are just not as good as you.

So, work out your next step, make sure there is someone to step into your shoes and the organisational world is your oyster!

PART **D**

DIRECTOR'S TOOLKIT

In Part B we introduced ten core tools and techniques that can be used from day one in your new role as a team leader or manager in your chosen field. As you progress up the career ladder to the role of senior manager, and as your team matures in terms of their understanding and capabilities, you will want to introduce more advanced or sophisticated techniques.

Part D provides a number of more sophisticated techniques developed and adopted by industry leaders – helping you to differentiate from your competitors.

	TOOL DESCRIPTION
T1	Team finance audit
T2	Financial ratio analysis
T3	Pareto profiling
T4	Risk analysis

T1 TEAM
FINANCE AUDIT

Use the following checklist to assess the current state of your team. Consider each criterion in turn and use the following scoring system to identify current performance:

0 Not done or defined within the business: unaware of its importance

1 Aware of area but little or no work done

2 Recognised as an area of importance and some work done in this area

3 Area clearly defined and work done in the area

4 Consistent use of best practice tools and techniques in this area

5 Area recognised as being 'best in class' and could be a reference area for best practice

Reflect on the lowest scores and identify those areas that are critical to success and flag them as status Red, requiring immediate attention. Then identify those areas that you are concerned about, and flag those as status Amber, implying areas of risk that need to be monitored closely. Green implies you are happy with the current state.

ID	CATEGORY	EVALUATION CRITERIA	SCORE	STATUS
F1	**Strategic fit**		**0–5**	**RAG**
A	Vision	There is a clear statement of corporate vision and strategy		
B	Goals	Senior and middle management have communicated the vision and strategy across the business by setting clear and attainable goals		
C	Congruence	The team members are committed to the goals set for them and understand how they fit in with the overall strategy		
F2	**KPI relevance**			
A	KPI cascade	There is a clear statement of the KPIs for both the team and individuals		
B	Briefing	The team is well briefed that if they achieve their KPIs they will be seen to be successful		
C	Contribution	The team's achievement of their KPIs makes a significant contribution to the organisation's goals and strategy		
F3	**KPI commitment**			
A	Understanding	Each member of the team understands their individual KPIs and the importance of team success		
B	Commitment	Each member of the team is committed to achieving their individual KPIs		
C	Support	When a team member is not hitting a KPI, they expect and receive support from managers in correcting the problem		
F4	**Basic knowledge**			
A	Cash flow	Each member of the team is aware of the crucial importance of cash flow management		
B	Income statement	Each team member understands the impact that their activities have on the income statement		
C	Balance sheet	The team members understand the difference between capital and revenue expenditure and how a balance sheet reflects this difference		

ID	CATEGORY	EVALUATION CRITERIA	SCORE	STATUS
F5	**Budgeting**		0–5	RAG
A	Process	The team understands the company's budgeting process and has a positive attitude towards it	☐	☐
B	Planning	The team is involved in producing the budget	☐	☐
C	Commitment	Each member of the team is committed to working with the budget	☐	☐
F6	**Financial research**			
A	Process	All members of the team are able to read an annual report and extract the data needed for analysis	☐	☐
B	Analysis	All members of the team can interpret the results of financial analysis of key customers, competitors and suppliers	☐	☐
C	Application	The team members use the results of financial analysis to improve their performance	☐	☐
F7	**Project evaluation**			
A	Comparison	The team understands that proposed projects will be analysed and compared with other proposals from elsewhere in the organisation	☐	☐
B	Template	The team understands the business case template that the organisation uses for evaluating proposed projects	☐	☐
C	Persuasive communication	The team is successful in presenting clear and cogent business cases		
F8	**Management accounting system**			
A	Understanding	The team understands the internal financial information system	☐	☐
B	Monitoring	The team uses the internal financial information system to monitor its performance	☐	☐
C	Improvement	Where the information system is weak, there is a plan in place to get the system improved	☐	☐

ID	CATEGORY	EVALUATION CRITERIA	SCORE	STATUS
F9	**Relationship with finance department**		0–5	RAG
A	Respect	The team respects the contribution that the finance department makes to the success of the organisation	☐	☐
B	Business environment	The financial controller understands the business environment in which the team is working	☐	☐
C	Coordination	The team keeps the finance department up to date with its performance and plans through regular communication	☐	☐
F10	**Analytic tools**			
A	Risk analysis	Each member of the team understands the techniques used to assess risk	☐	☐
B	Breakeven analysis	Each member of the team understands the methods of breakeven analysis	☐	☐
C	Decision making	Each member of the team understands the importance of using these analytic tools in decision making	☐	☐

T2 FINANCIAL RATIO ANALYSIS

One of the most useful capabilities a manager can develop is the ability to look beyond reported financial data and interpret key implications for their team and business – answering the 'So what?' question. Study the following three examples of statements for a major UK retailer and then review the financial ratios listed below.

Income statement example

The income statement shows the financial results of the transactions the company has made in the previous period of time. Companies produce income statements on a biannual or quarterly basis.

RETAIL GROUP PLC: INCOME STATEMENT FOR YEAR ENDED 31 DECEMBER		
	YEAR 2	YEAR 1
	£M	£M
Revenue	7,858.2	7,480.2
Cost of sales	−4,821.2	−4,570.0
Gross profit	**3,037.0**	**2,910.2**
Other income	43.3	57.6
Sales and marketing costs	−1,666.0	−1,549.7
Administrative expenses	−465.5	−508.8
Profit on property disposals	23.5	1.7
Operating profit	**972.3**	**911.0**
Finance income	56.1	29.4
Finance costs	−127.7	−124.6
Profit before taxation	**900.7**	**815.8**

RETAIL GROUP PLC: INCOME STATEMENT FOR YEAR ENDED 31 DECEMBER		
	YEAR 2	YEAR 1
	£M	£M
Income tax expense	−268.4	−241.7
Profit for the year	**632.3**	**574.1**
Attributable to:		
Equity shareholders of the parent	601.3	545.5
Minority interests	31.0	28.6
	632.3	574.1
Basic earnings per share (pence)	**45.8**	**38.8**
Diluted earnings per share (pence)	**45.1**	**37.7**
Notes to the accounts reveal the following further information:		
Depreciation	275.4	247.7
Dividends paid	299.3	227.0
Interest expense	127.7	98.1

Balance sheet example

The balance sheet shows the financial situation of the company at a moment in time. It deals with where the company's capital came from and how it has been deployed.

RETAIL GROUP PLC: BALANCE SHEET AS AT 31 DECEMBER		
	YEAR 2	YEAR 1
	£M	£M
ASSETS		
Non-current assets		
Property, plant and equipment	4,097.2	3,522.8
Goodwill	266.1	169.1
Investment property	21.8	21.9
Trade and other receivables	357.1	215.1
	4,742.2	**3,928.9**
Current assets		
Inventories	425.8	362.6
Trade and other receivables	267.9	171.3
Cash and cash equivalents	277.0	156.9
	970.7	**690.8**
Total assets	**5,712.9**	**4,619.7**
LIABILITIES		
Current liabilities		
Trade and other payables	850.6	909.2
Short-term borrowings	765.3	401.5
Current portion of long-term borrowings	5.4	3.8
Current tax payable	32.7	76.0
Short-term provisions	9.7	5.0
	1,663.7	**1,395.5**

RETAIL GROUP PLC: BALANCE SHEET AS AT 31 DECEMBER		
	YEAR 2	YEAR 1
	£M	£M
Non-current liabilities		
Long-term borrowings	1,686.7	1,075.2
Retirement benefit deficit	279.2	682.3
Trade and other payables	166.5	76.3
Long-term provisions	12.7	14.6
Deferred tax	324.1	6.4
	2,469.2	**1,854.8**
Total liabilities	**4,132.9**	**3,250.3**
Net assets	**1,580.0**	**1,369.4**
EQUITY		
Share capital	345.4	370.1
Share premium account	201.5	176.7
Other reserves	16.8	11.1
Retained earnings	1,009.9	810.1
Total shareholders' equity	**1,573.6**	**1,368.0**
Minority interests	6.4	1.4
Total equity	**1,580.0**	**1,369.4**
Notes to the accounts reveal the following further information:		
Trade receivables	73.7	59.1
Trade payables	197.6	226.2
Number of equity shares (millions)	1,381.8	1,480.4

Cash flow statement example

The cash flow statement identifies the flow of cash in and out of the business. It is related to the income statement, but will differ significantly in a number of ways.

RETAIL GROUP PLC: CONSOLIDATED CASH FLOW STATEMENT FOR YEAR ENDED 31 DECEMBER		
	YEAR 2	YEAR 1
	£M	£M
Cash flows from operating activities		
Profit before taxation	900.7	815.8
Adjustments for:		
Depreciation	275.4	247.7
Foreign exchange loss	6.2	3.4
Investment income	−43.3	−57.6
Interest expense	127.7	98.1
	1,266.7	**1,107.4**

RETAIL GROUP PLC: CONSOLIDATED CASH FLOW STATEMENT FOR YEAR ENDED 31 DECEMBER	YEAR 2	YEAR 1
	£M	£M
(Increase)/decrease in trade and other receivables	−238.6	76.3
(Increase)/decrease in inventories	−63.2	−56.9
Increase/(decrease) in trade payables	31.6	17.8
Cash generated from operations	**996.5**	**1,144.6**
Interest paid	−77.2	−107.1
Income taxes paid	−73.9	−64.4
Net cash inflow from operating activities	**845.4**	**973.1**
Cash flows from investing activities		
Acquisition of subsidiaries, net of cash acquired	−40.4	0.0
Purchase of property, plant and equipment	−805.3	−620.0
Interest received	54.1	32.3
Net cash outflow from investing activities	**−791.6**	**−587.7**
Cash flows from financing activities		
Buy back of equity shares	−464.4	−12.1
Proceeds from long term borrowings	830.0	301.6
Equity dividends paid	−299.3	−227.0
Net cash inflow from financing activities	**66.3**	**62.5**
Net cash inflow/(outflow) from activities	**120.1**	**447.9**
Opening net cash	156.9	−291.0
Closing net cash	277.0	156.9

Financial ratio analysis

Here are the ratios calculated from the data above.

Income statement ratios

It is the relationship between numbers on the income statement and balance sheet that allow you to gauge the financial health of a company. Here are the most commonly used ratios for the income statement and balance sheet above, with comments on their interpretation.

	FORMULA OR SOURCE	YEAR 2	YEAR 1	COMMENT
P/E ratio				
Share price (p)	From *Financial Times*, etc.	436.8		
Diluted EPS (p)	From foot of income statement	45.1		
P/E	Share price/ Diluted EPS	**9.7**		A fairly low P/E ratio, indicating that the market considers the share to be low growth
Yield				
Dividend per share (p)	Notes to accounts	21.7		
Share price (p)	From *Financial Times*, etc.	436.8		
Yield	Dividend per share/Share price	**5.0%**		A fairly high dividend yield. However, beware possible future cuts in dividend
				Note that P/E ratio and dividend yield are calculated based on the share price at the date of the calculation. There is no point in providing a calculation for the previous period
Dividend cover				
Diluted EPS (p)	From foot of income statement	45.1	37.7	
Dividend per share (p)	Notes to accounts	21.7	15.3	
Dividend cover	Diluted EPS/ Dividend per share	**2.08**	**2.46**	The large increase in dividend has resulted in reduced coverage. Cover of 2× is still safe but the shareholders need to keep an eye on this in the future
Return on sales				
Profit before taxation	Income statement	900.7	815.8	
Revenue	Income statement	7,858.2	7,480.2	
Return on sales	Profit before tax/ Revenue	**11.5%**	**10.9%**	Slightly improved performance

	FORMULA OR SOURCE	YEAR 2	YEAR 1	COMMENT
Return on assets				
Profit for year	Income statement	632.3	574.1	
Total assets	Balance sheet	5,712.9	4,619.7	
Return on assets	Profit for year/ Total assets	**11.1%**	**12.4%**	A major investment in fixed assets has not yet resulted in an increase to profits
Return on equity				
Profit for year	Income statement	632.3	574.1	
Shareholders' equity	Balance sheet	1,573.6	1,368.0	It is sometimes suggested that the figure for shareholders' equity should be the opening balance or the average balance
Return on equity	Profit for year/ Shareholders' equity	**40.2%**	**42.0%**	This would appear to be a very high return in both years. However, the measurement of shareholders' equity is based on capital introduced to the business plus retained realised profits. It is not the full value of the shareholders' investment, which would be the total market value of the company (see next ratio)
Return on market value				
Profit for year	Income statement	632.3		
Market value of the company	Number of shares × Share price	6,035.7		
Return on market value	Profit for year/ Market value of the company	**10.5%**		This is a more realistic estimate of the return earned by shareholders. It is simply a different way of calculating earnings per share. The reason that the figure is slightly different from that shown above is that the normal EPS calculation is based on diluted EPS, which uses a different number of shares in its calculation

	FORMULA OR SOURCE	YEAR 2	YEAR 1	COMMENT
Gross margin				
Gross profit	Income statement	3,037.0	2,910.2	
Revenue	Income statement	7,858.2	7,480.2	
Gross margin	Gross profit/ Revenue	**38.6%**	**38.9%**	A declining gross margin is a warning sign. It might mean that the company has to offer sales discounts to maintain turnover levels
Operating margin				
Operating profit	Income statement	972.3	911.0	
Revenue	Income statement	7,858.2	7,480.2	
Operating margin	Operating profit/ Revenue	**12.4%**	**12.2%**	In the light of the reduced gross margin, the operating margin has held up well – presumably due to close cost control
Net profit margin				
Profit for the year	Income statement	632.3	574.1	
Revenue	Income statement	7,858.2	7,480.2	
Net profit margin	Profit for the year/ Revenue	**8.0%**	**7.7%**	Solid but unspectacular

Balance sheet ratios

While the income statement ratios give a good view of recent performance, it is the balance sheet ratios that give the better clues to the long-
term history and potential of the company.

	FORMULA OR SOURCE	YEAR 2	YEAR 1	COMMENT
Current ratio				
Current assets	Balance sheet	970.7	690.8	
Current liabilities	Balance sheet	1,663.7	1,395.5	
Current ratio	Current assets/ Current liabilities	**0.58**	**0.50**	This is not unusual for a retailer, since inventory is usually converted into cash quickly enough to meet liabilities as they fall due

	FORMULA OR SOURCE	YEAR 2	YEAR 1	COMMENT
Quick assets				
Current assets	Balance sheet	970.7	690.8	
Inventory	Balance sheet	425.8	362.6	
Quick assets	Current assets – Inventory	**544.9**	**328.2**	
Quick ratio				
Quick assets	See above	544.9	328.2	
Current liabilities	Balance sheet	1,663.7	1,395.5	
Quick ratio	Quick assets/ Current liabilities	**0.33**	**0.24**	The quick ratio is quoted here because it is a commonly used measure of liquidity. It is designed to remove the slow-moving inventory from current assets so as to produce a stricter test of whether the company can meet its liabilities. It is not really relevant to retailers
Stock turn				
Cost of sales	Income statement	4,821.2	4,570.0	
Inventory	Balance sheet	425.8	362.6	
Stock turn	Cost of sales/ Inventory	**11.3**	**12.6**	A poor result for a retailer
Number of days of stock held				
Cost of sales	Income statement	4,821.2	4,570.0	
Inventory	Balance sheet	425.8	362.6	
Number of days of stock held	365 × Inventory/ Cost of sales	**32.2**	**29.0**	Another way of saying the same as the previous ratio. The retailer is holding about one month's stock
Debtors' days				
Revenue	Income statement	7,858.2	7,480.2	
Trade receivables	Notes to accounts	73.7	59.1	
Debtors' days	365 × Trade receivables/ Revenue	**3.4**	**2.9**	Most payments are in cash. Those that are not are typically on credit card. Debtors' days are always small for a retailer
Creditors' days				
Total expenses less depreciation	Income statement	6,677.3	6,380.8	
Trade payables	Notes to accounts	197.6	226.2	
Creditors' days	365 x Trade payables/ Expenses	**10.8**	**12.9**	Unusually generous

	FORMULA OR SOURCE	YEAR 2	YEAR 1	COMMENT
Income gearing				
Interest paid	Notes to accounts	127.7	98.1	
Operating profit	Income statement	972.3	911.0	
Income gearing	Interest paid/ Operating profit	**13.1%**	**10.8%**	The percentage of profits that need to be paid out as interest. The figure for this company is quite low and demonstrates that the company is not taking risks with borrowing
Total liabilities				
Non-current liabilities	Balance sheet	2,469.2	1,854.8	
Current liabilities	Balance sheet	1,663.7	1,395.5	
Total liabilities	May be available on balance sheet or may need to add the two totals above	**4,132.9**	**3,250.3**	
Debt to equity				
Total liabilities	See above	4,132.9	3,250.3	
Equity	Balance sheet	1,580.0	1,369.4	
Debt to equity	Total liabilities/ Equity	**261.6%**	**237.4%**	This is a measure of to what extent the company is financing itself from outside the business compared with funds provided by shareholders. This percentage is high and is growing: an area to watch
Total debt				
Short-term borrowings	Balance sheet	765.3	401.5	
Long-term borrowings	Balance sheet	1,686.7	1,075.2	
Current portion of long-term borrowings	Balance sheet	5.4	3.8	
Total debt (borrowings)	The sum of the above	**2,457.4**	**1,480.5**	
Total capital				
Total debt	See above	2,457.4	1,480.5	
Equity	Balance sheet	1,580.0	1,369.4	
Total capital	Total debt + Equity	**4,037.4**	**2,849.9**	

	FORMULA OR SOURCE	YEAR 2	YEAR 1	COMMENT
Debt to capital				
Total debt	See above	2,457.4	1,480.5	
Total capital	See above	4,037.4	2,849.9	
Debt to capital	Debt/Total capital	**60.9%**	**51.9%**	This is a similar measure to the above but now considers external finance in the form of formal borrowings. This ratio is normally known as gearing and any percentage over 50% is high gearing. It is interesting that the company has high gearing but seems to be well able to afford the interest payments out of earnings

T3 PARETO PROFILING

What is it?

Pareto profiling is a tool for analysing the true profitability of products, customers and suppliers.

Why use it?

As organisations develop, they often add new customers, products and activities, but they are often poor at stripping out unprofitable ones. This is made worse by the fact that most performance systems support the continuation of historic activities (i.e. salespeople are incentivised on sales – often without any true measure of how profitable the sales are). In addition, standard costing systems tend to hide the true profitability (or unprofitability) of areas of the business.

How do you use it?

So how do you start? Simply order your product list (or customers or suppliers) on a spreadsheet from high revenue (or contribution) to low revenue (or contribution) – with the highest at the top. This simple activity is often enough to get the team to think about two key issues:

1 **Why are we not focusing more on our most important products (or customers or suppliers) and finding ways to increase profitability?** Many organisations fail to treat their most important customers (or key accounts) differently. The rule of 80/20 suggests that 20% of your products or customers will deliver over 80% of your revenues.

2 **Why are we continuing to sell products (or deal with customers) that deliver such a small contribution to the bottom line?** Many products and customers will actually be unprofitable, since the rule of 50/5 suggests that the bottom 50% of your products or customers will deliver less than 5% of your revenues cumulatively (see figure). Just think what level of overhead cost is incurred in servicing this 'tail'. Pareto analysis such as 50/5 can be a great spur to taking a decision that would otherwise be shirked, such as cancelling a product set because of its low contribution.

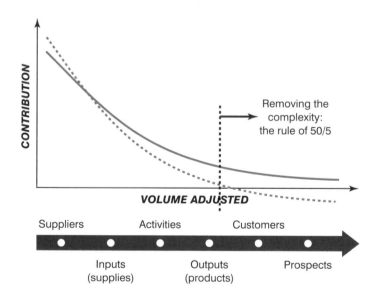

T4 RISK ANALYSIS

No estimate for the future will be exact; there will always be the unexpected, as well as the normal tolerance to be expected in a prediction. Before you produce the estimated profit and loss account, it is useful to take time out to look at the possible risks to the benefits and costs.

→ Risks to the benefits are that less than your prediction will occur, or that they will not occur in the timescale predicted.

→ Risks to the costs are that they will be greater than budget, either because your estimate is wrong or because delay has cost money.

We have already seen one of the ways of taking risk into account, which is to produce a range of forecasts: pessimistic, most likely and optimistic. Let's take that technique a step further.

Remember the types of benefit we identified. Here is another example of a risk matrix using the benefit type as the grouping:

	PESSIMISTIC	MOST LIKELY	OPTIMISTIC
Reduce costs	1	3	6
Avoid costs	2	5	8
Increase revenues or control	4	7	9

Experience allows us to give each cell in the matrix a number from 1 to 9. These numbers reflect the order of confidence that we have that the benefit will be achieved. Here, the order goes from the most likely to occur, 1, which is the pessimistic estimate for a cost reduction, to the least likely, 9, which is an optimistic estimate for a benefit in increased sales or improvement in control.

Assuming we know the costs involved in the project, we can now calculate whether this is a high- or low-risk project. Add up all the benefits from the cells marked 1 to 3. If that produces a number which is greater than the costs, the project can be termed low risk. If you have to go down to cell 8 or 9 before the costs are covered, you have a project that carries a high risk of not being profitable.

Don't forget that the objective of risk analysis is not only to identify what the risks are, but also to do something about them. If, for example, there was some doubt about the benefits in cell 5, and that doubt was the difference between a medium- and high-risk project, you might be inclined to do some more investigation to improve the estimate, or resolve to put extra resources into making sure that during the implementation of the project the benefits in that cell are actually realised.

A different, and very simple, way of ameliorating the risk of under-budgeting is to put contingency money into both the start-up costs of a project and the continuing revenue spend. Many companies build contingency into their investment appraisal technique as a norm. So, you have to put into the profit and loss account an extra 10% capital spend for contingency, and an extra 10% contingency on the running costs.

The final risk technique to mention is sensitivity analysis. Once you have used the net present value (NPV) method of financial appraisal you can use it to test the project by asking a series of 'What if …?' questions. For example, if you have the net present value figure of £1 million, you can take each uncertainty in the inputs and ask the following questions:

→ What is the effect on the NPV if this input changes?

→ How far can the input change before the NPV drops to zero?

Using this technique of sensitivity analysis helps to identify whether the project is likely to go wrong because of its sensitivity to key inputs. It also tells management which are the key inputs and therefore the ones to be most closely watched once the project is implemented.

THE FAST TRACK WAY

Take time to reflect

Within the Fast Track series, we cover a lot of ground quickly. Depending on your current role, company or situation, some ideas will be more relevant than others. Go back to your individual and team audits and reflect on the 'gaps' you identified, and then take time to review each of the top ten tools and techniques and list of technologies.

Next steps

Based on this review, you will identify many ideas about how to improve your performance, but look before you leap: take time to plan your next steps carefully. Rushing into action is rarely the best way to progress unless you are facing a crisis. Think carefully about your own personal career development and that of your team. Identify a starting place and consider what would have a significant impact on performance and be easy to implement. Then make a simple to-do list with timings for completion.

Staying ahead

Finally, the fact that you have taken time to read and think hard about the ideas presented here suggests that you are already a professional in your chosen discipline. However, all areas of business leadership are changing rapidly and you need to take steps to stay ahead as a leader in your field.

Take time to log in to the Fast Track web resource, at **www.Fast-Track-Me.com**, and join a community of like-minded professionals.

Good luck!

Other titles in the Fast Track series

This title is one of many in the Fast Track series that you may be interested in exploring. Whilst each title works as a standalone solution, together they provide a comprehensive cross-functional approach that creates a common business language and structure. The series includes titles on the following:

→ Strategy

→ Innovation

→ Project management

→ Sales

→ Marketing

GLOSSARY

accounting policies The specific principles, bases, conventions, rules and practices applied by an entity in preparing and presenting financial statements

accounts payable Amounts owed by the entity to suppliers and others who provide goods and services to the company. Also known as trade creditors

accounts receivable Amounts owed to the entity by customers and others. Also known as debtors

accrual An amount that the entity owes but which has not yet been recorded as a liability in the accounting records

accruals concept One of the fundamental principles on which accountancy is based. Amounts are recognised in the income statement in the period in which the transaction occurred, which is not necessarily the same as the period in which cash was received or paid

amortisation A charge made in the income statement each year which spreads the cost of an intangible asset over its expected useful life

arm's-length transaction A transaction between a willing buyer and a willing seller which takes place at a fair market value

assets Things an entity owns or has the use of. These may include property, equipment, patents, inventory, receivables and cash

audit An examination by a suitability qualified person or firm who is independent of the company. Note, internal audit also exists, which is an examination performed by an employee of the company

auditors' report A report prepared by the auditors which is issued with the company's financial statements. It normally follows a standard format, stating that the accounts show a true and fair view (or setting out any modifications to that opinion)

balance sheet A statement at a particular point in time showing what the entity owns (its assets), what it owes (its liabilities) and the difference between them, which is the shareholders' equity

capital expenditure Expenditure on non-current assets such as buildings or equipment

cash equivalents Short-term, highly liquid investments that are readily convertible to cash

cash flow Inflows and outflows of cash and cash equivalents

consolidated financial statements The financial statements of a group presented as those of a single economic entity

contingent liability A possible obligation that arises from past events and whose existence will be confirmed only by the occurrence or non-occurrence of one or more uncertain future events not wholly within the control of the entity. An entity should disclose a contingent liability except when the possibility of a payment being required is remote

convertible A financial instrument that can be converted into equity shares

cost of goods sold See *cost of sales*

cost of sales The costs associated with buying or producing the items which have been recorded as sales in the income statement. If the entity produces goods, then cost of sales will include a fair proportion of the manufacturing overheads of the entity. Also known as cost of goods sold

current assets Assets that will be sold, used up in production or realised into cash within 12 months after the balance sheet date

current liabilities Liabilities that are due to be settled within 12 months after the balance sheet date

depreciation A charge made in the income statement each year which spreads the cost of a tangible asset over its expected useful life

discontinued operations A major component of an entity that either has been disposed of or is classified as held for sale

dividends Distributions of profits to holders of equity investments in proportion to their holdings of a particular class of capital

earnings per share The profit for the year divided by the number of shares in issue

EBITDA An acronym for earnings before interest, taxes, depreciation and amortisation. This is a measure commonly used by analysts

equity The residual interest in the assets of the entity after deducting all its liabilities. This is known as shareholders' funds in the accounts of unquoted companies that are following UK accounting standards

fair value The amount for which an asset could be exchanged, or a liability settled, between knowledgeable, willing parties in an arm's-length transaction

financial statements Usually comprise a balance sheet, income statement, statement of cash flows, a statement of changes in equity and notes to the accounts

fixed assets See *non-current assets*

fixed costs Expenses that do not vary with the level of sales or output

generally accepted accounting practice (GAAP) Rules for financial reporting that are either embodied in accounting standards or have grown up as accepted practice

going concern The assumption that the entity will continue in operation for the foreseeable future with neither the intention nor the necessity to liquidate or materially curtail its scale of operations

goodwill account The difference between the amount paid to purchase a business and the fair value of the separable assets acquired. Goodwill arises as a result of factors that cannot be measured in figures, such as reputation, customer base or staff experience

gross profit Revenue less cost of sales

income statement A statement showing revenues and expenses over a period of time. Also known as a profit and loss account or P&L

initial public offering (IPO) The first time a company's shares are offered for sale on the stock market

intangible assets Identifiable, non-monetary assets without physical substance, such as a licence or patent

International Accounting Standards Board (IASB) A body that establishes accounting standards. These standards are followed by companies in over 100 countries around the world, including all European listed companies

liabilities Obligations of the entity arising from past events, which will require settlement by an outflow of resources

liquidity The availability of sufficient funds to meet financial commitments as they fall due

limited company A separate legal entity formed for the purpose of operating a business. The shareholders' liability is limited to any amount outstanding on their shares

long-term liabilities See *non-current liabilities*

material misstatement An error that has a significant impact on an entity's financial position

net assets Total assets less total liabilities

net book value The cost (or valuation) of non-current assets less accumulated depreciation

net profit Gross profit less all expenses

net sales or net revenue Sales revenue less deductions for items such as sales discounts

non-current assets Assets held for use in the business, such as plant, property, equipment and patents. Known as fixed assets in UK GAAP

non-current liabilities Financial obligations that are not due for payment within 12 months of the balance sheet date. Known as long-term liabilities in UK GAAP

notes to the financial statements The section in the annual report that gives more information about the financial performance and position of the entity

operating cash flow Cash generated by operations, as distinct from cash generated by investing or financing activities

ordinary share A share that normally gives the right to participate in profits and the right to vote at meetings

parent company A company that controls one or more other companies

partnership An unincorporated business owned by more than one person

preference share A share that normally gives a right to a fixed dividend. Dividends are not guaranteed but must be paid before dividends can be paid to ordinary shareholders. A preference share

may sometimes be redeemable. It does not normally give a right to vote at meetings

profit The difference between the revenues earned in the period and the costs incurred in earning them. However, profit can be described in a number of ways, such as gross profit, operating profit or net profit, and these terms have different meanings

profit and loss account (P&L) See *income statement*

provision A liability of uncertain timing or amount. A company should recognise a provision in the financial statements when it is more likely than not that a payment will be required to settle the obligation

recognition The process of incorporating in the balance sheet or income statement an item that meets the definition of revenue, expense, asset or liability

related party A party can be related to an entity in a number of ways, including where they: a) control the entity; b) are members of the same group of companies; c) are a member of key management personnel of the entity; d) are a close family member of a) or c) above. Two parties are also related if they are subject to common control

related party transaction A transaction between related parties. Related party transactions are disclosed in financial statements because of the risk that they may be not at arm's length

retained earnings Profit that is not paid out to shareholders in the form of dividends

revenue Payments received for the sale of products or supply of services

royalties Payments made for the use of intellectual property owned by another company or individual

secured debt Money borrowed on the basis of security

shareholders' funds See *equity*

sole proprietorship An unincorporated business owned by an individual

solvency A company's ability to pay its debts

statement of cash flows One of the primary financial statements. It reports the sources and uses of cash during a period

tangible assets Assets with physical form, such as equipment or property

trade debtors See *trade receivables*

Trade receivables Amounts owed to the entity by customers. Also known as trade debtors or accounts receivable

turnover Revenue received from sales

unrealised losses or gains Changes in the value of an asset owned by the entity

variable costs Costs that change based on the level of sales or output

wholly owned subsidiary A company whose shares are all owned by another company – the parent company

working capital Current assets less current liabilities

INDEX

Items in **bold** relate to entries in the Glossary

FAST TRACK TO SUCCESS

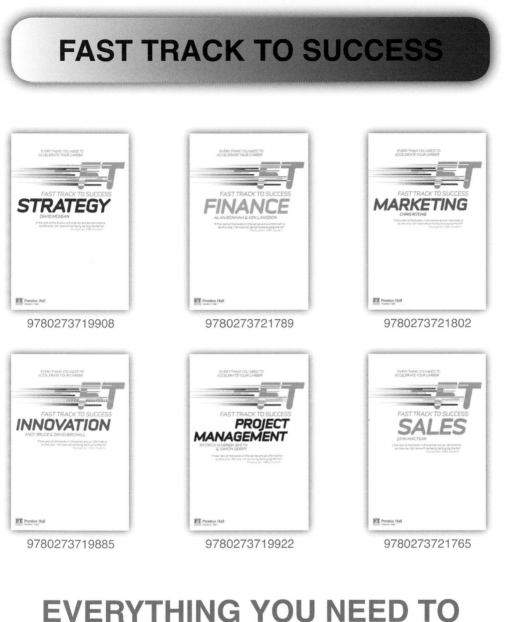

9780273719908

9780273721789

9780273721802

9780273719885

9780273719922

9780273721765

EVERYTHING YOU NEED TO ACCELERATE YOUR CAREER

FT Prentice Hall
FINANCIAL TIMES